THE PASSENGERS AND CREW OF THE TITANIC

FRANCESCO • CHAFFEE, CARRIE TOOGOOD • CHAFFEE, HERBERT FULLER • CHAMBERS, BERTHA GRIGGS • CHAMBERS, NORMAN CAMPBELL • C[...] CHARLES H. • CHAPMAN, J. • CHAPMAN, JOHN HENRY • CHAPMAN, SARAH ELIZABETH LAWRY • CHARBOISSON, ADRIAN • CHARMAN, JOHN [...] WILLIAM • CHERRY, GLADYS • CHEVERTON, W. F. • CHEVRE, PAUL ROMAINE • CHIBNALL, EDITH MARTHA BOWERMAN BARBER • GHIP, CHANG • CHISHOLM, RODERICK ROBERT • CHISNALL, GEORGE ALEXANDER • CHITTY, G. • CHORLEY, J. • CHRISTMANN, EMIL • CHRISTMAS, H. • CHRISTY, ALICE FRANCES • CHRISTY, JULI R. • CHRONOPOULOS, APOSTOLOS • CHRONOPOULOS, DEMETRIOS • CLARK, VIRGINIA McDOWELL • CLARK, WALTER MILLER • CLARK, WILLIAM • CLARKE, ADA MARIA WINFIELD • CLARKE, CHARLES VALENTINE • CLARKE, JOHN FREDERICK PRESTON • CLARK, THOMAS • CLEAVER, ALICE MARY • CLENCH, FREDERICK • CLENCH, GEORGE • CLIFFORD, GEORGE QUINCY • COE, HARRY • COELHO, DOMINGOS FERNANDES • COHEN, GERSHUN (GUS) • COLBERT, PATRICK • COLEFF, FOTIO • COLEFF, PEYO • COLEMAN, ALBERT EDWARD • COLEMAN, JOHN • COLERIDGE, REGINALD CHARLES • COLGAN, JOSEPH • COLLANDER, ERIK • COLLETT, SIDNEY C. STUART • COLLEY, EDWARD POMEROY • COLLINS, JOHN • COLLINS, SAMUEL • COLLYER, CHARLOTTE ANNIE TATE • COLLYER, HARVEY • COLLYER, MARJORIE LOTTIE • COMPTON, ALEXANDER TAYLOR JR. • COMPTON, MARY ELIZA INGERSOLL • COMPTON, SARA REBECCA • CONLIN, THOMAS HENRY • CONNAGHTON, MICHAEL • CONNER, J. • CONNOLLY, KATE • CONNOLLY, KATE • CONNORS, PATRICK • CONWAY, P. W. • COOK, C. • COOK, GEORGE • COOK, JACOB • COOK, SELENA ROGERS • COOMBES, C. • COOMBES, GEORGE • COOPER, HARRY • COOPER, JAMES • COPPERTHWAITE, B. • COR, BARTOL • COR, IVAN • COR, LUDOVIK • CORBEN, ERNEST THEODORE • CORBETT, IRENE COLVIN • CORCORAN, DENNIS • COREY, MARY PHYLLIS ELIZABETH MILLER • CORN, HARRY • CORNAIRE, MOREL • CORNELL, MALVINA HELEN LAMSON • COTTERILL, HARRY • COTTON, A. • COUCH, FRANK • COUCH, J. • COUPER, R. • COUTIN, AUGUSTO • COUTTS, MINNIE • COUTTS, NEVILLE • COUTTS, WILLIAM LESLIE • COX, WILLIAM DENTON • COXON, DANIEL • COY, FRANCIS EDWARD GEORGE • CRABB, H. • CRAFTER, F. • CRAFTON, JOHN BERTRAM • CRAWFORD, ALFRED • CREASE, ERNEST JAMES • CREESE, HENRY PHILIP • CRIBB, JOHN HATFIELD • CRIBB, LAURA MARY • CRIMMINS, JOHN • CRISP, ALBERT HECTOR • CRISPIN, WILLIAM • CROSBIE, J. BERTRAM • CROSBY, CAPT. EDWARD GIFFORD • CROSBY, CATHERINE ELIZABETH HALSTEAD • CROSBY, HARRIET R. • CROSS, W. • CROVELLA, LOUIS • CROWE, GEORGE FREDERICK • CRUMPLIN, CHARLES • CULLEN, CHARLES • CUMINGS, FLORENCE BRIGGS THAYER • CUMINGS, JOHN BRADLEY • CUNNINGHAM, ALFRED FLEMING • CUNNINGHAM, ANDREW • CUNNINGHAM, B. • CURTIS, A. • CURTIS, ARTHUR • DAHER, TANNOUS • DAHL, KARL (CHARLES) EDWARD • DAHLBERG, GERDA ULRIKA • DAKIC, BRANKO • DALY, EUGENE • DALY, MARCELLA • DALY, PETER DENIS • DANBOM, ANNA SIGRID MARIA BROGREN • DANBOM, ERNST GILBERT • DANBOM, GILBERT SIGVARD EMANUEL • DANIEL, ROBERT WILLIAMS • DANIELS, SARAH • DANIELS, SIDNEY ALBERT • DANOFF, YOTO • DANTCHOFF, KHRISTO • DASHWOOD, WILLIAM G. • DAVIDSON, ORIAN HAYS • DAVIDSON, THORNTON • DAVIES, ALFRED J. • DAVIES, CHARLES HENRY • DAVIES, EVAN • DAVIES, GORDON RALEIGH • DAVIES, JOHN SAMUEL • DAVIES, JOHN JAMES • DAVIES, JOSEPH • DAVIES, ROBERT J. • DAVIES, THOMAS • DAVIS, AGNES MARY FRIGGENS • DAVIS, JOHN MORGAN • DAVIS, MARY • DAVIS, STEPHEN J. • DAVISON, MARY E. FINCK • DAVISON, THOMAS HENRY • DAWSON, JAMES • de BRITO, JOSE JOAQUIM • DE MESSEMAEKER, ANNA • DE MESSEMAEKER, WILLIAM JOSEPH • DE MULDER, THEODORE • DE PELSMAEKER, ALPHONSE • DEACON, PERCY WILLIAM • DEAN, BERTRAM FRANK • DEAN, BERTRAM VERE • DEAN, ELIZABETH GLADYS MILLVINA • DEAN, EVA GEORGETTA LIGHT • DEAN, GEORGE H. • DeBREUCQ, MAURICE EMIL • DEEBLE, ALFRED ARNOLD • DEL CARLO, ARGENE GENOVESI • DEL CARLO, SEBASTIANO • DELALIC, REGYO • DENARCISSIO, GIOVANNI • DENBUOY, HERBERT • DENNIS, SAMUEL • DENNIS, WILLIAM • DERRETT, A. • DESLANDS, PERCY • DESVERNINE, LOUIS • DEVANEY, MARGARET • deVILLIERS, BERTHE ANTONINE (MAYNE) • DEWAN, FRANK • DIAPER, J. • DIBDEN, WILLIAM • DIBO, ELIAS • DICK, ALBERT ADRIAN • DICK, VERA GILLESPIE • DICKSON, W. • DILLEY, JOHN • DILLON, THOMAS PATRICK • DiMARTINO, GIOVANNI • DIMIC, JOVAN • DINENAGE, JAMES K. • DINTCHEFF, VALTCHO • DOBBIN, JAMES* • DODD, EDWARD CHARLES • DODD, GEORGE CHARLES • DODDS, RENNEY WATSON • DODGE, DR. WASHINGTON • DODGE, RUTH VIDAVER • DODGE, WASHINGTON • DOEL, FREDERICK • DOLBY, JOSEPH • DOLING, ADA JULIA • DOLING, ELSIE • DONATI, ITALO • DONOGHUE, T. • DOOLEY, PATRICK • DORE, A. • DORKINGS, EDWARD ARTHUR • DORNIER, LOUIS • DOUGHTY, N. • DOUGLAS, MAHALA DUTTON • DOUGLAS, MARY-HELENE "SUZETTE" BAXTER • DOUGLAS, WALTER DONALD • DOUTON, WILLIAM JOSEPH • DOWDELL, ELIZABETH • DOYLE, ELIZABETH • DOYLE, L. • DRAPKIN, JENIE • DRAZONOVIC, JOSEF • DREW, JAMES VIVIAN • DREW, LULU THORNE CHRISTIAN • DREW, MARSHALL BRINES • DRISCOLL, BRIDGET • DUFFY, WILLIAM LUKE • DULLES, WILLIAM CROTHERS • DUNFORD, W. • DUQUEMIN, JOSEPH • DURAN Y MORE, ASUNCION • DURAN Y MORE, FLORENTINA • DYER, HENRY RYLAND • DYER, WILLIAM • DYKER, ADOLF FREDRIK • DYKER, ANNA ELIZABETH JUDITH ANDERSSON • DYMOND, JOHN • EAGLE, A. J. • EARNSHAW, OLIVE POTTER • EASTMAN, CHARLES • ECONOVIC, JOSO • EDBROOKE, F. • EDE, GEORGE B. • EDGE, FREDERICK WILLIAM • EDVARDSSON, GUSTAF HJALMAR • EDWARDS, C. • EGG, W. H. • EITEMILLER, GEORGE FLOYD • EKLUND, HANS LINUS • EKSTROM, JOHAN • ELIAS, ELIAS • ELIAS, JOHN • ELIAS, JOSEPH • ELLIOTT, EVERETT EDWARD • ELLIS, J. R. • ELSBURY, WILLIAM JAMES • EMANUEL, VIRGINIA ETHEL • ENANDER, INGVAR • ENDRES, CAROLINE LOUISE • ENNIS, WALTER • ERVINE, ALBERT GEORGE • ETCHES, HENRY SAMUEL • EUSTIS, ELIZABETH MUSSEY • EVANS, ALFRED FRANK • EVANS, EDITH CORSE • EVANS, FRANK OLIVER • EVANS, GEORGE • EVANS, GEORGE • EVANS, W. • EVERETT, THOMAS JAMES • FAHLSTROM, ARNE JONAS • FAIRALL, H. • FARENDEN, ERNEST • FARQUHARSON, WILLIAM EDWARD • FARRELL, JAMES • FARTHING, JOHN • FAULKNER, WILLIAM STEPHEN • FAUNTHORPE, HARRY • FAUNTHORPE, MRS. HARRY (IN REALITY, MRS. ELIZABETH A. WILKINSON) • FAY, THOMAS JOSEPH • FELLOWS, J. ALFRED • FELTHAM, GEORGE • FENTON, THOMAS • FERRARY, ANTON • FEY, CARLO • FILLBROOK, CHARLES J. • FINCH, HARRY • FINOLI, LUIGI • FISCHER, EBERHARD TELANDER • FITZPATRICK, CHARLES WILLIAM N. • FITZPATRICK, HUGHJ • FLARTY, E. • FLEET, FREDERICK • FLEGENHEIM, ANTOINETTE • FLEMING, MARGARET • FLETCHER, PETER W. • FLYNN, JAMES • FLYNN, JOHN IRVING • FLYNN, JOHN • FOLEY, JACK • FOLEY, JOSEPH • FOLEY, W. C. • FOLEY, WILLIAM • FOO, CHOONG • FORD, ARTHUR • FORD, DOOLINA MARGARET (DAISY) • FORD, ERNEST WATSON • FORD, ERNEST • FORD, F. • FORD, H. • FORD, MARGARET ANN WATSON • FORD, ROBINA MAGGIE (RUBY) • FORD, THOMAS • FORD, WILLIAM NEAL • FOREMAN, BENJAMIN LAVENTALL • FORTUNE, ALICE ELIZABETH • FORTUNE, CHARLES ALEXANDER • FORTUNE, ETHEL FLORA • FORTUNE, MABEL • FORTUNE, MARK • FORTUNE, MARY McDOUGALD • FORWARD, J. • FOSTER, A. • FOX, PATRICK • FOX, STANLEY HUBERT • FOX, WILLIAM THOMAS • FRANCATELLI, LAURA MABEL • FRANKLIN, ALAN VINCENT • FRANKLIN, CHARLES (IN REALITY, CHARLES FARDON) • FRANKLIN, THOMAS PARNHAM • FRASER, J. • FRASER, JAMES • FRAUENTHAL, CLARA HEINSHEIMER • FRAUENTHAL, DR. HENRY WILLIAM • FRAUENTHAL, ISAAC GERALD • FREDERICKS, W. • FREEMAN, ERNEST EDWARD SAMUEL • FROLICHER, HEDWIG MARGUERITE • FROLICHER-STEHLI, MARGRIT EMERENTIA STEHLI • FROLICHER-STEHLI, MAXMILLIAN JOSEF • FROST, ANTHONY W. • FRY, JOHN RICHARD • FRYER, A. • FUNK, ANNIE CLEMMER • FUTRELLE, JACQUES • FUTRELLE, MAY PEEL • FYNNEY, JOSEPH J. • GALE, HARRY • GALE, SHADRACH • GALLAGHER, MARTIN • GALLOP, F. • GARDENER, F. • GARFIRTH, JOHN • GARSIDE, ETHEL • GASKELL, ALFRED • GATTI, LUIGI GASPARE • GAVEY, LAWRENCE • GEDDES,

RMS TITANIC, INC.

Today, more than eighty-six years since *Titanic* departed from Southhampton on her maiden voyage, we are proud to participate in the largest showing of the objects of *Titanic*, through *TITANIC: The Exhibition.*

The night of April 14, 1912, was one of the saddest moments in history. Scholars often refer to Shakespeare and the literature of ancient Greece to express the magnitude of *Titanic*'s sinking, yet no one but those who walked on *Titanic*'s decks can truly speak to the events of that fateful night. As these voices fade, so does the memory of *Titanic*.

We at RMS Titanic, Inc. believe it is imperative for all of us to preserve the story of *Titanic* for current and future generations. It is our duty to ensure that the story of *Titanic* does not become a myth in the decades and centuries to come. The objects of *Titanic*, carefully recovered and conserved through great effort, will remain the most vital and strong witness to the reality of *Titanic*.

RMS Titanic, Inc. was founded to preserve the memory of *Titanic*. The *Titanic* artifact collection is one of the world's most astonishing collections, containing more than five thousand objects that have been carefully selected on the basis of diversity, message, and voice. This collection is representative of the peoples of more than forty nations. It helps us to appreciate and share our common heritage, and to attempt to understand the enormity of *Titanic*'s loss.

We appreciate this opportunity to express our deepest gratitude to all of the countless people and institutions around the world who have labored endlessly and tirelessly to help us realize our goal of sharing these objects with the world. We hope *Titanic*'s objects and this thoughtful exhibition will allow you time to reflect on *Titanic*'s many legacies. From all of us at RMS Titanic, Inc., we wish to thank the survivors and their families who have helped us so greatly, and we wish to extend our thanks to each of you who visit this exhibition for helping us to preserve *Titanic*'s memory.

January 1, 1999
RMS Titanic, Inc.
New York, New York

In 1996, the City of Saint Paul hosted "America's Smithsonian" for thirty-one days. Over 450,000 people viewed America's great cultural, historical, and artistic treasures in the Saint Paul Civic Center. More than 100,000 Minnesota school-children experienced the great heritage of their past, and most certainly understood their responsibility for the future.

Today, Media Rare, Inc. is pleased to produce, in conjunction with RMS Titanic, Inc., *TITANIC: The Exhibition*. This rich and rewarding exhibition places in context the story of the world's most famous ship and its most famous tragedy.

Thanks to the efforts of so many individuals, organizations, and companies, *TITANIC: The Exhibition* will be housed in a locally famous facility—The Saint Paul Union Depot Concourse. For the first time in nearly thirty years, thousands of people will be able to encounter a monumental exhibition in the sturdy elegance of the concourse.

For Minnesotans, the poignancy of the experience could not be more striking. Nearly one-third of the passengers on the *Titanic* were Scandinavians bound for a new life in a new land. As visitors experience *TITANIC: The Exhibition*, they will be met with the echoes of the thousands of immigrants who entered the doors of the Union Depot Concourse, ready to start a new life in America—and the haunting memory of the ill-fated Scandinavian passengers who never made it through those depot gates.

All of us at Media Rare, Inc. are proud of our association with *TITANIC: The Exhibition*. It is a pride built upon our commitment to present to you the most expansive, beautiful, and thought-provoking experience possible. We have spared no effort to ensure that your experience and time in the Saint Paul Union Depot Concourse is one that remains with you for a lifetime.

Michael F. Priesnitz
President/CEO
Media Rare, Inc.

Erich E. Mische
Executive Vice President
Media Rare, Inc.

The legendary saga of Titanic *is a story known the world over. But for the four of us, who personally lived through that tragedy, it is more than a story— it is a moment in time when our lives were forever changed. In that moment, we became inextricably linked to one another and to* Titanic.

TITANIC: The Exhibition *provides the public with the opportunity to experience the tragic story of* Titanic—*the sensitive and respectful display of objects recovered and conserved from the great ship. As survivors of this disaster, we are pleased to see the memories of the ship and of the loved ones we lost so long ago preserved in such an accurate and dignified manner.*

Millvina Dean

Michel Navratil

Edith Haisman

Eleanor Shuman

Edith Haisman passed away on January 20, 1997 at the age of 100.

Eleanor Shuman passed away on March 6, 1997.

*To the men, women, and children who lost their lives in the waters of the North Atlantic
on the night of April 14, 1912; to those who survived—whose lives from that night
on were forever altered; and to those who built the Titanic,*

*May the pages of this book succeed in conveying the magnitude of the world's loss as a result of the
tragic sinking of the Titanic. And may they convey the significance of the continuing scientific
study of the Titanic on the ocean floor and the concerted efforts of many to conserve and
preserve all that can be rescued from the wreck site.*

*May all of these efforts help safeguard our world from future maritime disasters and
ensure that the memory of the Titanic is never forgotten.*

To you—the passengers, crew, and builders of the Titanic—this book is respectfully dedicated.

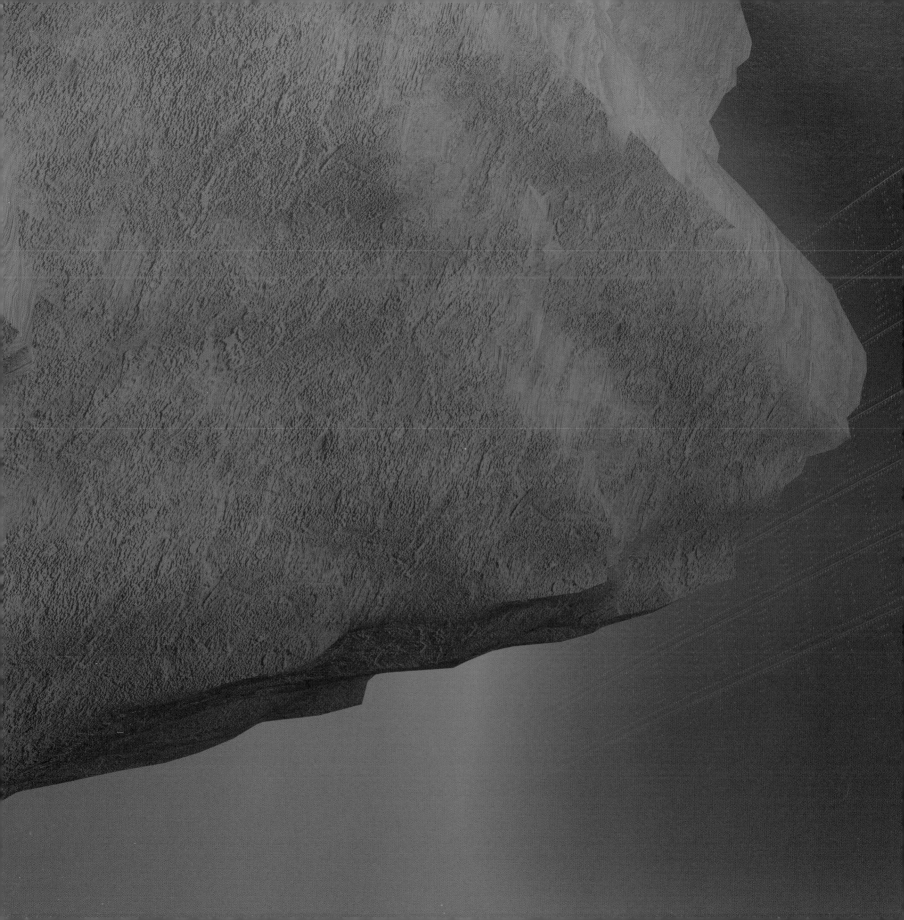

TITANIC

LEGACY OF THE WORLD'S GREATEST OCEAN LINER

BY SUSAN WELS

TIME
LIFE
BOOKS

DISCOVERY
CHANNEL

ACKNOWLEDGMENTS

I am extremely grateful to everyone who offered me their generous assistance and support in the preparation of this book.
Most of all, I owe deep thanks to my father, Richard H. Wels, who was born the year after the Titanic *sank and who,*
in so many ways, was the guiding spirit for this book. I am also profoundly indebted to Allan Carlin, a dear friend whose vision,
persistence, and sheer optimism inspired and infused this project. Tom Lewis, Chris Capen, Andy Lewis, Nancy Cash, Laura
Georgakakos, and the entire Tehabi team were, as always, a joy to work with. George Tulloch, Matt Tulloch, Jack Eaton, and Charlie
Haas provided indispensable help and were immensely generous with their time and expertise. I am especially indebted to Elizabeth
Perle McKenna, David Cohen, and Devyani Kamdar for their guidance and to Christy Tripp for her research assistance. I owe thanks
to my husband, David Hagerman, and to our daughters, Emily and Casey, for their endless love and patience.
Susan Wels—*San Francisco, California*

TEHABI BOOKS

Titanic was conceived and produced by Tehabi Books.

Managing Editor	Nancy Cash
Copy Editor	Laura Georgakakos
Art Director	Andy Lewis
Webmaster	Sam Lewis
Editorial Assistant	Sarah Morgans
Editorial and Design Director	Tom Lewis
Controller	Sharon Lewis
President	Chris Capen

Additional support for *Titanic* was provided by

Image Resourcing	Bill Broyles
Copy Proofer	Jeff Campbell
Technical Editors	John P. Eaton and
	Charles A. Haas
Passenger and Crew Listings	Michael Findlay

Library of Congress Cataloging-in-Publication Data
Wels, Susan–1956–
    Titanic: legacy of the world's greatest ocean liner.
    p. cm.
    "Preface by William F. Buckley"—Jacket.
    Includes bibliographical reference and index.
    ISBN 0-7835-5261-0
    1. Titanic (Steamship) 2. Shipwrecks—North Atlantic Ocean.
G530.T6T58 1997
910'.916'4—dc21   97-16404
10 9 8 7 6 5 4 3 2   CIP

TIME® LIFE BOOKS

Time-Life Books is a Division of Time Life Inc.

TIME LIFE INC.

PRESIDENT and CEO	George Artandi

TIME-LIFE BOOKS

PRESIDENT	Stephen R. Frary

TIME-LIFE CUSTOM PUBLISHING

VICE PRESIDENT AND PUBLISHER	Terry Newell
Vice President of Acquisitions and Executive Editor	Kate Hartson
Associate Publisher	Teresa Hartnett
Vice President of Sales and Marketing	Neil Levin
Director of Marketing	Inger Forland
Director of New Product Development	Quentin McAndrew
Director of Editorial Development	Jennifer Pearce
Director of Special Sales	Liz Ziehl
Managing Editor	Donia Ann Steele
Research	Kimberly A. Grandcolas

TIME-LIFE is a trademark of Time Warner Inc. USA

Books produced by TIME-LIFE Custom Publishing are available at
special bulk discount for promotional and premium use.
Custom adaptations can also be created to meet your specific
marketing goals. Call 1-800-323-5255.

Photo captions pages: **xxii.** Ship's bell. **xxi.** Leaving Belfast. **xix.** Steaming across the Atlantic. **xvii.** The *Titanic's* hull scrapes against the iceberg. **xv.** Survivors in lifeboats watch the great ship go down. **xiii.** The launching of *Nautile*. **xi.** *Nautile* descends to the wreck site. **x.** View of the wreckage. **ix.** The ship's telegraph on the ocean floor. **viii.** View of the wreckage. **vii.** The *Titanic* propeller. **iv.** The *Titanic* three days before sinking. **iii.** Men dwarfed by the hull of the triple screw steamer.

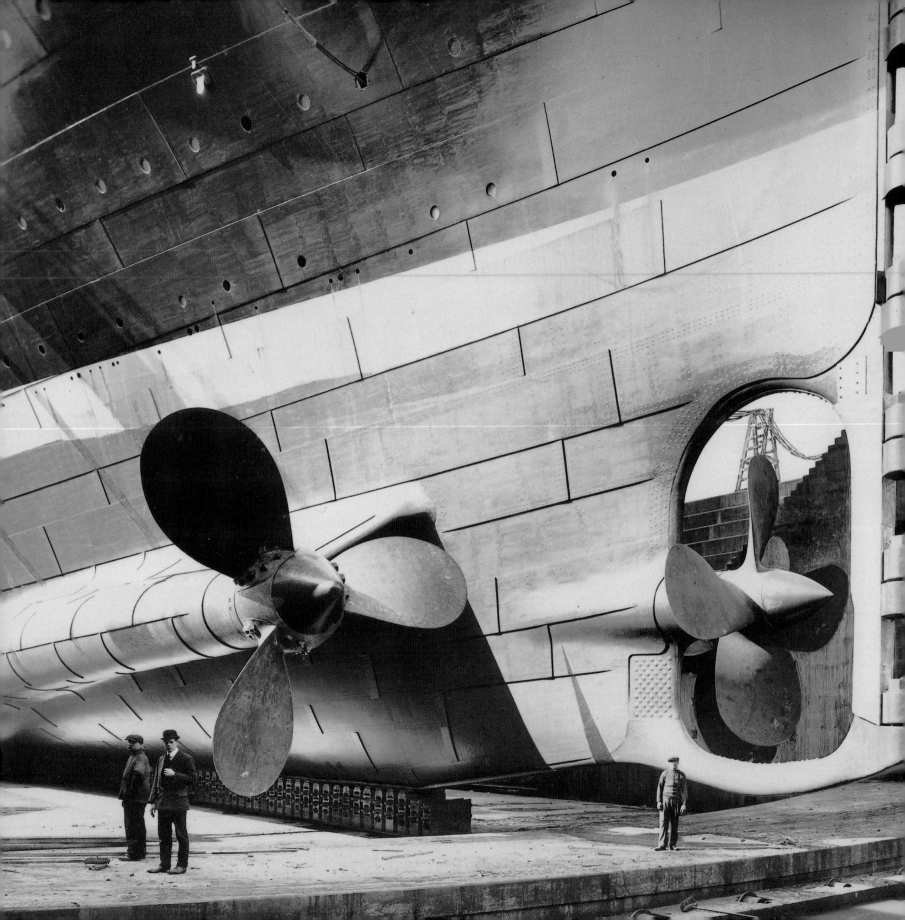

CONTENTS

ON THE OCEAN FLOOR

A teacup, perhaps the personal property of a *Titanic* passenger. Left: A view of the anchor attached to the hull of the *Titanic*.

THE TENDER VESSEL IS bound for the spot where the *Titanic* sank on the night of April 14, 1912. Along with a crew of fifty-three, it carries aboard a half dozen of the scientists and entrepreneurs who make up the joint U.S. and French expedition devoted to studying the wreck site and recovering artifacts from the floor of the ocean, two and a half miles beneath the ocean's surface. There is tension, as one might expect diving deep into the ocean, but there is also a different tension because this is the *Titanic*.

Although it has been eighty-five years since it went down, and there are only a few survivors of that haunted night still living, the *Titanic* is widely thought of as an international monument, incorruptible in its chaotic arrangements on the ocean floor.

For this reason, great tenderness is shown toward the White Star's glamorous, ill-fated vessel. There has been no manhandling of the ghostly carapace, and divers in a tiny submersible with prehensile arms and a marsupial front have been bringing up only loose-lying artifacts that would otherwise have continued to rest on the ocean floor.

Since 1987, four summer-long expeditions have brought this team to the *Titanic* because it won't be long before the wreck deteriorates entirely into an indiscernible mound of debris on the ocean floor.

At eleven in the morning, 963 miles northeast of New York City, 453 miles south of Newfoundland, after being asked one final time whether I suffered from claustrophobia, I am directed to the shoulder-wide opening of the little submarine, leading to vertical iron railing steps descending into the tubular control center of the *Nautile*. A $25 million underwater exploratory vessel built with titanium, the *Nautile* is 6 feet in diameter at its widest point and weighs only 18 tons. The chief pilot occupies the berth on the port side. Behind him, sitting on an abbreviated chair, is the copilot. The starboard berth is for the "observer," in this case me. Each of us has a porthole built of one-foot-thick plastic. The copilot, in addition, has two sets of 8-inch television screens. The first set looks ahead via remote video, one camera trained to look dead ahead, the other to pivot. The second set of videos portrays at close range and at longer range the exact operation of the mechanical arms operating from either side of the *Nautile*, designed to pick up objects from the seabed. With aid of the video, the operator can exactly instruct the arms.

To descend the two and a half miles to the ocean floor takes ninety minutes. I try to sit up, which requires me to raise my knees six inches or so—there is no room to stretch them out. I was advised not to eat breakfast, and dutifully I did not. There are moments when you wonder whether an extra million dollars might not have been dredged up to add a few cushions.

But the great moment is coming. We will reach the bottom and Georges, our pilot, will turn on the outside beams. We are in place,

▲

William F. Buckley, Jr., prepares to explore the *Titanic* wreck site aboard IFREMER's *Nautile*.

standing by our portholes. The lights flash on. Nothing to see, though the water is startlingly clear, diaphanous to the extent of our light's beam, an apparent twenty-five to thirty feet ahead, never mind that it is pitch dark out there.

Then, gradually, it happens: We descend slowly to what looks like a yellow-white sandy beach, sprinkled with black rock-like objects. These, it transpires, are pieces of coal. There must be a hundred thousand of them in the area we survey, between the bow and the stern.

Just off to the right a few feet, a snow-white teacup. Just sitting there, thank you, on the sand. I liken the sheer neatness of the tableau to a display that might have been prepared for a painting by Salvador Dalí.

We proceed ahead, looking for three specific objects previously photographed: one of them a man's valise; the second, a part of a leaded window, missing from the larger window now reconstructed; and the third, the loose-lying control levers that had fallen from the bridge, from which the captain had ordered the engines shut down after the iceberg was hit.

My job is to constantly strain my eyes to the right, lest we glide by the objective. And to direct the attention of Georges to any object I think especially interesting. My problem is that I find everything especially interesting. But soon I come to know when to bid legitimately for the attention of Georges and when simply to think, Forget it. Just one more teacup from the *Titanic*.

We are below, searching and scooping, for six and one-half cold hours. But the sensation, in microcosm, is vivid, exhilarating, and uncomplicated by any philosophical misgivings about our mission. I am a passive part of an archaeological venture that is also an adventure—only about 150 men and women in the world have dived as deep in the water as I am now. The excavation is singular because it is being conducted in a part of the planet heretofore thought totally inaccessible.

Finally, the moment comes to terminate our sortie, to begin our slow ascent. After a few minutes, permission is requested over the radio (permission granted) to jettison one of our two lead-weight ballasts, permitting a sharp increase in our rate of ascent.

I try to sit up, just to find something different to do with my bones. But I have to lean just slightly forward. Otherwise, I might lean just slightly back, in which case I might brush up against one of those hundred toggle switches behind me and, who knows, flip the one that will toss me out with the teacups— the pressure out there is 6,000 pounds per square inch.

I look for the one-hundredth time at the fast-changing depth meter. This time it joyfully tells me that we have just about reached

▲

The three-man submersible can reach a maximum depth of 20,000 feet on dives up to twelve hours long.

the surface. It seems an age before the frogmen are there to secure us to the halyard coming down from the ship's crane. But eventually we are airborne into the mother ship's womb. The hatch is turned and I climb out, a Superman grin on my face, I have to admit.

So, what comes from all these efforts? Before I left on this adventure, I was contemplating the question, When does the focus change? When do you put down the glasses that see only tales of distress and suffering and pick up the other set, which focuses on science and history, on surviving artifacts— the sort of things that bring us to museums for whatever reason? Because they are beautiful, or because they are unique, or because they are intimately associated with a great historic event.

What happened on that night in April was certainly all those things. No one will deny it. The research and recovery efforts therefore refresh the legend of the *Titanic*, they make possible scientific and historic discoveries, they preserve artifacts for public exhibit so that future generations will be cautioned in their pursuit of extrahuman conceits. And, among other things, they consumed ten days of my time—willingly given and abundantly rewarded.

William F. Buckley, Jr.

"Our lifeboat, with thirty-six in it, began lowering to the sea. This was done amid the great confusion. Rough

seamen all giving different orders. No officer aboard. As only one side of the ropes worked, the lifeboat

at one time was in such a position that it seemed we must capsize in mid-air. At last the ropes worked

together, and we drew nearer and nearer the black, oily water. The first touch of our lifeboat on that black sea

came to me as a last good-bye to life, and so we put off—a tiny boat on a great sea—rowed away from what

had been a safe home for five days. The first wish on the part of all was to stay near the Titanic.

We all felt so much safer near the ship. Surely such a vessel could not sink. I thought the danger must be

exaggerated, and we could all be taken aboard again. But surely the outline of that great, good ship was

growing less. The bow of the boat was getting black. Light after light was disappearing. . . ."

Elizabeth Shutes, First-Class Passenger

TITANIC

▲

This intricately etched sterling silver cufflink box was recovered from the wreck site. Its cloth-lined interior still held several pairs of cufflinks as well as a woman's bobby pins and hat pin. Left: The *Titanic* sets off on her maiden voyage.

HER NAME IS PUBLICLY announced in April 1908. The laying of keel blocks for Yard No. 401—her builders' designation—begins on March 31, 1909. During the ensuing two years, parts and plating and pieces come from all parts of the globe to be assembled into the world's mightiest ship: steel from Scotland; teak from Siam; fabrics from Holland; the immense rudder and stern castings from Darlington, Durham. From the world over to the Harland and Wolff shipyard at Belfast, Ulster—parts for an Irish ship, built by Irish workers.

Her strength and classic beauty would astound the world. Her sad fate would become the world's grief. Her name . . . *TITANIC.*

While the *Titanic* lies at Southampton taking aboard cargo and supplies, carpenters, painters, and plumbers work feverishly to complete a number of cabins prior to the sailing date, while belowdecks an ominous condition has developed. Due to the coal strike, *Titanic* was unable to take aboard fuel at Belfast from a single source, so coal from several vessels was loaded into the new liner's bunkers. In the number 10 bunker of the aft starboard side of the number 6 boiler room, the spontaneous ignition has occurred, and even before the liner's Belfast departure, the coal is smoldering. Round-the-clock shifts of trimmers are assigned to control the fire, shoveling away the top layers to get at the glowing embers beneath. Chief engineer Joseph Bell, who joined the ship at Belfast, and his staff are fully aware of the condition: his daily reports at both Belfast and Southampton Bell *must* have notified Captain Smith as well. Plans for taking on cargo and for on-time departure are not modified. Even though the fire continues up to and past sailing time, there is no public record or report of the occurrence.

April 10, 1912—a gusty Wednesday at Southampton, with bright clouds scudding across a sunlit sky. By 10 A.M. the crew is mustered, and the lifeboat drill (boats 11 and 15 are lowered, floated and raised) is over. The Board of Trade inspection of muster lists and safety devices is completed. The *Titanic* is ready to receive passengers.

Workers loaded 5,892 tons of coal aboard the *Titanic* for her maiden voyage. Due to a coal miners' strike, several liners relinquished their coal to fill the *Titanic*'s bunkers. She burned 690 tons per day. Several thousand tons of coal remain scattered across the debris field.

Boarding the liner for her maiden voyage is a true cross-section of Victorian/Edwardian society: aristocrat, millionaire, gentleborn; merchant, teacher, artist; servant, laborer, farmer. The *Titanic*'s passenger manifest is as varied as the multilayered societies on both sides of the Atlantic.

The ship triumphantly departs her Southampton mooring on time, at 12:15 P.M. The departure's sheen is somewhat tarnished by a slight incident involving a near collision, moments after leaving the dock, between the *Titanic* and the liner *New York*, moored nearby. Extricating the immense liner from her difficulty and enabling her to steam away occupies the better part of an hour. Her rendezvous with history is now only about ninety-five hours away.

The *Titanic* and her appointments provide enjoyment and a sense of security for all aboard. Her comforts would have been unknown to passengers of *any* shipboard class as recently as two decades ago—gentle music and soft lights, cuisine to tempt all palates, open deck spaces for strolling or relaxing.

High on the forward navigating bridge, far from intrusion by passengers or unauthorized crew, the *Titanic*'s captain, Edward John Smith, and his staff of seven officers look after the liner's navigation and operation. Plotting and maintaining the ship's course is perhaps their

The *Olympic* (left) and her sister ship the *Titanic* (right) in one of the few instances when they were afloat together. This photograph was taken in the outer berths of the Harland and Wolff shipyards in Belfast, Ireland. The *Titanic* was being fitted out and the *Olympic* had returned to the yards for repairs to a propeller. Lower right: A gold telescopic pencil recovered from the wreck site bears the inscription "R.L.B. Xmas 1908."

most important function. But their duties also include maintaining the quality of life aboard ship and providing for the vessel's overall safety. Though all the officers have been selected for their competency and accomplishment in the company's service, the ultimate responsibility for *all* administrative and navigational functions lies with the ship's captain.

As the *Titanic* makes a sweeping port turn around Ireland's southernmost coast and heads out into the Atlantic's gentle swells, Captain Smith no doubt experiences a sensation of pride mingled, perhaps, with an almost unconscious twinge of apprehension.

It is his *duty* to know that there has been a coal fire smoldering up to and past sailing time in bunker number 6; it is his *duty* to know that the ship's watertight compartmentalization and bulkhead heights are insufficient to keep his vessel afloat under certain circumstances; it is his *duty* to know that there are lifeboat seats sufficient for only 1,178 of the 2,228 passengers and crew aboard; it is his *duty* to heed the warnings of ice along his course that will soon be relayed by wireless from other ships.

Yet, in the end, E. J. Smith ignored

▲ Nearly 5,000 objects have been recovered from the *Titanic* debris field. Clockwise from top: Safe door from the purser's office; chandelier from a first-class public room; a five-dollar bill; a silver-plated serving dish made especially for use in first class aboard the *Olympic* and *Titanic*.

these facts, or at least relegated them to the back of his mind, as perhaps the commander of any North Atlantic passenger liner of 1912 would have done. Smith's duty was to the ship and her passengers. But his greater duty was to the company, to the owners and managers of the White Star Line—to avoid harming the ship and its contents and to bring the vessel into port on schedule. By speeding *Titanic* through the dark, moonless night, Captain Smith at least partially fulfilled that greater duty to the company. But by disregarding—however unconsciously—his duty to the ship and its passengers he initiated events of cataclysmic consequence.

Of the events that followed the *Titanic*'s fatal encounter with an iceberg on the night of April 14–15, 1912, much has been written, much pondered. Deeds of heroism and cowardice, episodes of terror and tragedy, inspiring moments of unselfish sacrifice, all have been chronicled, all have been considered and interpreted.

What emerges is the paradox that the *Titanic* was concurrently one of the darkest moments in maritime history and one of the brightest. Though soon displaced by the Great War's awesome terror, the *Titanic*'s loss changed forever the way humans considered themselves, their environment, and their relation to Nature. The disaster also brought about the development of many significant safety measures still in use today and whose benefits will extend into the future.

Today, many decades after her loss, the grace and glory of the *Titanic*'s beauty also promises to extend into the future. Following the wreck's discovery in 1985, several scientifically-oriented expeditions have devoted time and pioneering effort to the recovery of objects from the sea's floor adjacent to the wreck, two and a half miles below the North Atlantic's surface. Handled and regarded by the recovery crew with respect bordering on reverence, the objects are initially stabilized aboard the recovery vessel; after being landed, they are taken to the LP3 Conservation Laboratory at Semur-en-Auxois, a thirteenth-century French village where, subjected to centuries-old techniques as well as cutting-edge technologies, the objects are lovingly and skillfully conserved and preserved.

The objects open a window to history. They permit the viewer to look through and better understand the *Titanic*, her people, and her times. Recent recoveries and scrutiny have enabled scientists to understand the wreck in detail and formulate answers to hitherto unfathomable mysteries of the disaster's causes and effects.

Without the inspiration and leadership of two extraordinary men, Paul-Henri Nargeolet and George Tulloch, the *Titanic*'s legacy might have been lost at sea forever rather than preserved and protected. Sharing their efforts are the divers, the crew, and the technicians of the French research vessel *Nadir* and the operators of the submersible *Nautile*. Risking their lives on an almost daily basis, these men and women participate in a camaraderie of exploration and achievement seldom equalled in modern enterprise.

Paul-Henri Nargeolet and George Tulloch recognize the burden placed on them by History. RMS Titanic, Inc.—the company that financed, organized, and directed the recovery efforts—observes its responsibility to preserve the *Titanic*—her beauty as well as her story for all generations.

The *Titanic*'s hull lies rusting on the sea floor. Soon, in a generation, possibly two, corrosion and bacterial activity shall take their toll. The wreck shall no longer exist. Myth and legend will replace fact and reality. But because of the dreams and perseverance of those in our own time, we shall now and always have before us, preserved for all time, the beauty and integrity of a graceful liner's enduring significance.

John P. Eaton and Charles A. Haas

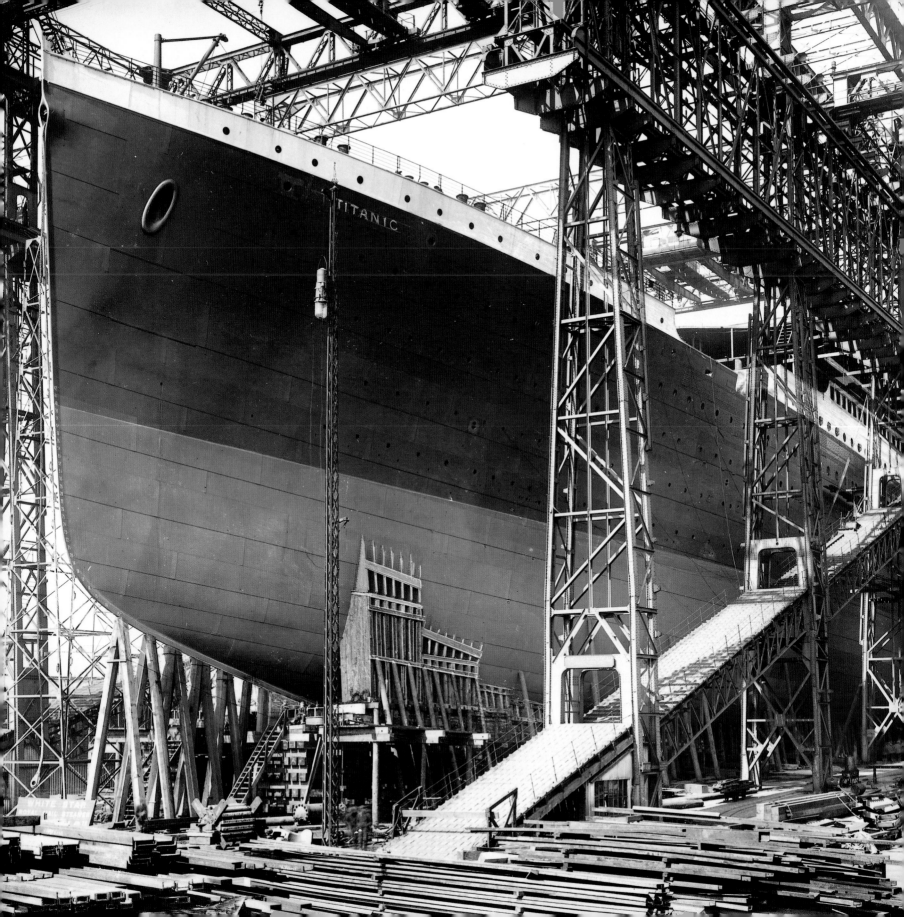

THE TIME OF THE TITANIC

▲

An 18-karat gold pocket watch, perhaps belonging to one of the *Titanic*'s first-class passengers, was found at the bottom of the North Atlantic. Left: The *Titanic* under construction in Belfast.

THE NORTH ATLANTIC, EVEN in the mild months, is a cruel, bad-tempered sea. Wild hurricanes howl across her icy, gray-green waters. Blinding fogs ravage the sky, and gales shriek violently from the north and west. Icebergs thunder to the sea, cracked from the frozen wastes of Greenland, then float like deadly drifting islands south past Labrador to the Grand Banks. It was in the spring, in April, on a calm, still, moonless night, that the great White Star liner the *Titanic*, on her maiden voyage to New York in 1912, sped across the quiet North Atlantic into a massive barricade of ice. Suddenly, almost silently, an iceberg scraped her starboard side. And within three hours, the immense, luxurious *Titanic* had disappeared beneath the ocean, carrying 1,523 passengers and crew members—millionaires and emigrants, men, women, and children—to their freezing deaths. The tragic loss of the *Titanic*, the greatest ship the world had ever seen, was proof, once more, of the dangers of the North Atlantic passage— perils that the *Titanic*, overconfidently, had been designed to overcome.

The hazards and discomforts of the crossing were especially notorious in the early nineteenth century, when ships began to hurtle passengers and mail across the furious Atlantic according to fixed schedules, heedless of the vicious storms, wind, and ice that lay ahead. The grueling voyages could take a month or more and were frequently a terrible ordeal. Steerage passengers, packed into unsanitary quarters, struggled to survive starvation and the deadly contagions that often killed dozens before the ship steered into port. Even for first-class passengers, the crossing was often a misery because of crowding, poor food, and the total lack of ventilation belowdecks. Being on a ship, Samuel Johnson once commented, "is being in a jail, with the chance of being drowned." Most people dreaded and feared ocean voyages, with good reason; as many as sixteen out of every hundred ships never reached port or mysteriously disappeared without a trace.

Later, in the early days of steam navigation, the North Atlantic passage could still be a nightmarish experience. Charles Dickens crossed from Liverpool to Boston in 1842 aboard Cunard's Royal Mail Ship *Britannia* and wrote this dreary account: "Before descending into the bowels of the ship, we had passed from the deck into a long and narrow apartment not unlike a gigantic hearse with windows in the sides." Of the berths, he lamented, "nothing smaller for sleeping in was ever made except coffins." There were few places for passengers to gather aside from the cramped dining saloon, a confining ladies' cabin, and the upper deck, where gentlemen could attempt some conversation surrounded by crates and poultry coops. According to Mark Twain, the ships offered no place to smoke except a repulsive den made of rough boards; there were no seats; and "the seas broke in through the cracks every little while and drenched the cavern thoroughly." Fresh milk was supplied to women, children, and invalids by an unfortunate seagoing cow, who was kept in a padded deckhouse.

▶

The *Olympic* under construction in the Harland and Wolff shipyards, Belfast, Ireland. The *Titanic* is barely visible at the left edge of the scene.

But thanks to new shipbuilding designs and robust competition, the transatlantic experience vastly improved between 1859 and 1900—so much so that modern liners could transport passengers and mail across the perilous Atlantic in just one week, in unimagined luxury. Ocean-going steamships had become magnificent floating hotels equipped with every device for the safety, comfort, and amusement of passengers. By 1906, a British naval architect could boast that "we may, without exaggeration, liken the saloons of our best ocean liners to the halls of kings' palaces."

By the first decade of the twentieth century, an optimistic age, modern transatlantic liners were also believed to be practically impervious to the perils of the sea. The march of progress, it was believed, would soon make ocean voyages nearly as safe as a holiday in a seaside luxury resort. By 1911, new marine technologies, from watertight compartments to schemes that used compressed air to keep water out of ships, were touted as making the most modern vessels "unsinkable"—a word that found its way into both newspaper headlines and conservative shipbuilding journals. "We have come to believe," the *New York Times* editorialized, "that our great modern liners, with their water-tight compartments, safeguarded by unceasing vigilance and rigid discipline, are secure against loss by collision, that even after the most violent shock they will be kept afloat."

Many of the travelers crossing the Atlantic in the new seagoing palaces were rich, free-spending Americans, Britons, and Europeans who shuttled back and forth between the continents during the carelessly extravagant Gilded Age.

By the late 1890s, Germany's fast, luxurious ships were challenging Britain's domination of the profitable transatlantic passenger trade. The *Kaiser Wilhelm der Grosse* won the coveted Blue Riband for speed in 1897 by steaming across the Atlantic at 22.5 knots. Other fast German liners quickly followed, including *Kronprinz Wilhelm, Kaiser Wilhelm II*, and *Kronprinzessin Cecilie*. Britain's Cunard Line responded to German competition in 1907 by introducing two luxurious new liners—the legendary, 31,000-ton *Lusitania* (pictured above) and the *Mauretania*—which reached record-setting speeds of 26 to 28 knots.

Nearly fifteen thousand yardworkers (left) were employed to build the *Olympic* and *Titanic*—the largest moving objects that had ever been constructed. The *Titanic* is visible in the background in the left gantry. Above: To accommodate the giant liners, Harland and Wolff removed three existing slipways from its Queens Island, Belfast, yards and replaced them with two huge new slips, specially reinforced with steel and a massive layer of concrete 4-1/2-feet thick. Towering above them was a new 175-foot gantry, the largest ever erected in the world. Right: When the *Titanic* sailed on her maiden voyage, her crew included an engineering staff with nine of the best engineers and draughtsmen from the Harland and Wolff yards. This wrench from the *Titanic* was recovered from the bottom of the ocean.

Known as a "triple screw steamer" because it was driven by a combination of three cast steel and bronze propellers, the *Titanic* (previous spread) and the *Olympic* (above) featured gigantic wing propellers that were over 23 feet in diameter and a center propeller that spanned more than 16 feet.

Left: The center anchor of the *Olympic* and *Titanic* weighed 15 1/2 tons. Each enormous ship required three anchors to restrain it.

Accustomed to luxury, pursued by society columnists, and accompanied by personal maids and valets, some had made as many as sixty Atlantic crossings in their lives. But belowdecks, in less elegant and well-appointed quarters, were masses of emigrants who had scraped together savings for the ocean passage to a new homeland in America—men, women, and children of little means who, by their sheer numbers, were swelling the passenger lists and profits of the Atlantic steamship companies.

Shipping firms competed vigorously to capture both classes of trade. The established British lines—Cunard, formed in 1839, and the younger White Star Line, purchased by Thomas Henry Ismay in 1867—dominated the lucrative North Atlantic run until the 1890s, when they faced increasing competition, especially from the German shipping lines. Nevertheless, Britain's fast, comfortable passenger steam-ships captured the biggest share of North Atlantic traffic, ferrying more than 9 million people between 1891 and 1911. Though her supremacy was increasingly being challenged, Great Britain ruled the waves. A fifth of the world's population lived under her dominion, her naval fleet was the most formidable in the world, her shipyards produced half of the world's merchant marine vessels, and she was determined to protect her lead against the rival

▲

The *Titanic*'s passengers spend their final on-shore moments before boarding. For many emigrants who sailed on the *Titanic*'s maiden voyage, the trip to America promised to be the fulfillment of a dream, offering the chance of a new life.

Germans by producing the biggest, fastest, and most comfortable ships afloat.

It was Britain's White Star Line that had first set new standards for steamship comfort and design with the launch of its Oceanic in 1870—a ship that featured, among other innovations, roomy cabins complete with running water. Soon after, the company's *Britannic* and *Germanic*, completed in 1874 and 1875, enhanced White Star's growing reputation by achieving new speed records, crossing the Atlantic in fewer than seven and a half days at a pace greater than 16 knots. White Star then bettered that performance with its *Teutonic* and *Majestic*, launched in 1889, which reached cruising speeds as high as 20 knots.

By the late 1890s, however, Germany had decisively entered the transatlantic race with a slew of luxurious liners that set new records for speed. Not to be outdone by the upstart Germans, Britain's Cunard threw down the gauntlet in 1907 by introducing two enormous and magnificent new ships, the legendary, 31,000-ton *Lusitania* and *Mauretania*. Driven by advanced turbine engines and four propellers, the remarkable new ships proudly reclaimed the speed record for Britain with their record-setting pace of 26 to 28 knots, enabling the liners to dash across the North Atlantic in fewer than five days.

The *Titanic*'s twenty-nine boilers, each 15 feet 9 inches in diameter, were constructed by Harland and Wolff. Left: A forward launching cradle held the *Titanic* in place until she was ready to be released into the water. Opposite page: On May 31, 1911, the *Titanic* was launched into the River Lagan, still without her four majestic funnels. Following spread: After launching, the *Titanic* spent ten months being fitted out and furnished in Harland and Wolff's deep-water basin.

While Cunard took on competitors in speed, White Star set out to surpass rivals in the comfort of its ships and the elegance of their appointments. Even on this score, however, its challenger Cunard had the obvious advantage. The *Lusitania* and *Mauretania* were considerably more spacious than White Star's largest and newest ship, the 24,541-ton *Adriatic*. Clearly, White Star's management knew, bold action was needed. The best chance for White Star to bolster its weakening competitive position was to do what no passenger line had ever done before—build a trio of astounding superships that would, by their almost unimaginable size and elegance, dwarf and eclipse all other vessels.

* * *

ONE EVENING IN THE spring of 1907, while the *Lusitania* and *Mauretania* were nearing completion, J. Bruce Ismay, White Star's chairman and managing director, met for dinner at the London home of Lord William James Pirrie, chairman of the renowned shipbuilding firm Harland and Wolff. Together, the two men laid decisive plans. White Star would indeed build three gigantic ships, Ismay and Pirrie decided—each 50 percent larger and 100 feet longer than the new Cunard goliaths. Weighing in at a stupendous 45,000 tons, the leviathans would not only be the largest ships afloat—they would be the largest moving objects ever made by

▲ **A**merican millionaire J. P. Morgan was a guest of honor at the *Titanic*'s launch—not as a spectator but as owner of the stupendous ship. Morgan had bought the White Star Line in 1902, hoping to profit on the Atlantic passenger trade, and he added it to his huge International Mercantile Marine (IMM) consortium of shipping companies. Construction of the magnificent liner was funded by an issue of IMM stock. Although Morgan had booked passage on the *Titanic*'s maiden voyage, business affairs forced him to cancel his plans.

man. Their vastness would be equalled by the unrivaled lavishness and variety of their appointments, calculated to attract the most pampered first-class passengers. Although the giant ships were not intended to set speed records, cruising at a moderate clip of 22 to 23 knots, travelers would cross the Atlantic in unmatched safety and comfort within a week, without the annoying vibration that commonly afflicted faster vessels. All three of the new liners would be built at Harland and Wolff's Belfast shipyards. Their names would be the Royal Mail Ships *Olympic*, *Titanic*, and *Gigantic*.

Construction work began on December 16, 1908, when the keel of the first leviathan, the *Olympic*, was laid down at the Harland and Wolff shipyards. The keel of her younger sister, the *Titanic*, was laid several months later, on March 31, 1909. One by one, the massive frames of the giants gradually emerged, looming over the River Lagan and every structure in the Belfast yards. Soon, an observer wrote, "the skeleton within the scaffolding began to take shape, at the sight of which men held their breaths. It was the shape of a ship, a ship so monstrous and unthinkable that it towered there over the buildings and dwarfed the very mountains by the water. . . . A rudder as big as a giant elm tree, bosses and bearing of propellers the size of windmills—everything was on a nightmare scale. . . . "

The *Titanic* carried sixteen wooden lifeboats and four collapsible boats on her spacious boat deck. Although the ship had lifesaving capacity for 1,178 people—less than half the 3,547 passengers and crew she was designed to carry—she surpassed lifeboat requirements by over 17 percent. Right: This sand-cast bronze bench end, recovered from the ocean bottom, once adorned the *Titanic*'s boat deck.

THE GRAND STAIRCASE

Since 1870, Harland and Wolff had been responsible for every detail of White Star liners, from hulls and machinery to the ornate carved paneling that adorned the walls of first-class cabins and reception rooms. There was never an agreed-upon price; Harland and Wolff's commission was simply to build the best possible ships. Left: On the *Olympic* and *Titanic*, first-class passengers were surrounded by the most lavish possible appointments, including the magnificent after grand staircase. Below: The forward grand staircase was crowned by a luminous glass dome. Lower left: A piece of intricately carved railing from the grand stairway was found floating in the Atlantic Ocean a few days after the *Titanic* sank. Right: This bronze cherub, recovered from the wreck site in 1987, may have come from the area of the *Titanic*'s after grand staircase. Below right: The clock from the elaborate grand staircase.

The immensity of the ships was nearly inconceivable to many of the nearly fifteen thousand yardworkers who riveted, forged, and hammered the great liners into being. The hull of each "monster of the sea" was made of more than two thousand one-inch-thick steel plates, held together by more than 3 million steel rivets. The double-bottomed hulls each weighed 26,000 tons and stretched 882 feet—nearly three football fields in length—from end to end. Because of their tremendous mass, each colossus required three anchors to restrain it. The center anchor alone, at 15 tons, needed a team of horses to transport it. A single link in the gigantic anchor chains weighed in at 175 pounds. The enormous rudder, the height of a house, weighed 20,250 pounds. Steam to drive each ship was generated by twenty-four double-ended and five single-ended boilers, each huge enough to contain a double-decker tramcar. And each of the superships was powered by the latest advances in marine engineering—an innovative, efficient combination of a turbine and the most powerful steam reciprocating engines ever built. This propelling machinery was so immense that it took the strength of three men to lift a single nut for connecting engine bolts.

Work proceeded quickly on the ships, and on October 20, 1910, the *Olympic* was at last ready to be launched into the

▲
This telegraph from the *Titanic*, used to communicate desired speed from the ship's officers to the engine room, was recovered in 1987.

River Lagan. Seven months later, on the warm, sunny morning of May 31, 1911, the *Titanic* followed her sister into the river. She was the largest and most wondrous vessel ever built, a thousand tons bigger than the *Olympic*. To watch her historic launch, more than a hundred thousand spectators crowded the shipyard and clung to nearby rooftops, masts, and river banks, straining to see the gargantuan ship released into the water. Distinguished visitors were present, too. On a special VIP viewing stand, decked out with red and white bunting for the occasion, J. Bruce Ismay and Lord Pirrie were joined by notables including the Lord Mayor of Belfast and John Pierpont (J. P.) Morgan, the American railroad, coal, and steel titan. As the eager crowd waited and British and American flags fluttered from the giant gantry beside the White Star pennant, workers knocked away, one by one, the wooden supports that held the *Titanic* to her slip. To ease her immense bulk into the water, workers had greased the 750-foot sliding way with 22 tons of slick tallow, oil, and soap. Finally, a red flag was raised, warning rockets shot up in the sky, whistles shrieked, and at thirteen minutes past noon, the immense hydraulic triggers that secured the colossus were released. Sixty-two seconds later, the *Titanic* slid quickly and quietly into the water of the River Lagan.

The great, much-anticipated event had ended, and the VIPs retired to a lunch hosted by Lord Pirrie at the Grand Central Hotel. But for

The *Titanic* featured a gymnasium packed with the latest athletic equipment, including mechanical bicycles, "camels," and "horses." Left: First-class passengers on the *Olympic* could work off rich meals by exercising with a punching bag.

THE LARGEST STEAMERS IN THE WORLD
WHITE STAR LINE

"OLYMPIC"
(IN SERVICE JUNE, 1911)

882½ FEET LONG
92½ FEET BROAD
45,324 TONS REGISTER
66,000 TONS DISPLACEMENT

HEIGHT FROM KEEL
TO TOP OF FUNNELS
175 FEET

"TITANIC"
(IN SERVICE APRIL, 1912)

882½ FEET LONG
92½ FEET BROAD
45,000 TONS REGISTER
66,000 TONS DISPLACEMENT

HEIGHT FROM KEEL
TO TOP OF FUNNELS
175 FEET

Sectional View
(AMIDSHIP)
THE TRIPLE SCREW SEA GIANTS
"OLYMPIC"   "TITANIC"
IN SERVICE JUNE, 1911   IN SERVICE APRIL, 1912

THE TITANIC'S SPECIFICATIONS

Length	882 ft. 9 in.
Height (waterline to boat deck)	60 ft. 6 in.
Extreme Breadth	92 ft. 6 in.
Distance from keel to funnel	175 ft.
Gross Tonnage	46,329
Net Tonnage	21,831
Horsepower (reciprocating engines)	30,000
Horsepower (turbine engine)	16,000 shaft
Cruising speed	23 to 24 knots
Launch Date	May 31, 1911
Maiden Voyage	April 10, 1912

A model of the *Titanic* beautifully conveys her graceful lines and grandeur. Upper left: An early poster details the building specifications and tonnage of the White Star Line's newest "sea giants," the *Olympic* and *Titanic*. The cutaway image on the poster shows the various features of each deck. Notice the saltwater swimming pool, and the tennis and handball courts on the middle F deck. A "small world within" was how the French science fiction writer Jules Verne described the interior of a steamship.

the *Titanic*, the work was just beginning. Her empty hull, not yet sporting its four majestic funnels, was towed to Harland and Wolff's deep-water basin. There, for ten months, she was fitted out with engines, boilers, and other mechanical equipment. Craftsmen adorned her with stained-glass windows, rich carpeting, elaborate chandeliers, and magnificently carved paneling. Nothing of the scale and luxury of the *Titanic* and *Olympic* had ever been seen before. In a special edition devoted to the immense new sister ships, the prestigious industry journal *The Shipbuilder* reported that the greatest pains were being taken "to provide passenger accommodation of unrivalled extent and magnificence," and the excellent result "defies improvement." Other ships may have featured impressive decor, but the *Olympic* and *Titanic* literally redefined the modern shipboard experience. They were the very first ocean liners to pamper their passengers with the novelty of an on-board squash court. In addition to a swimming pool, they each had a gymnasium fully equipped with the latest athletic equipment from Wiesbaden—including mechanical bicycles, "camels," and "horses." A sumptuous Turkish bath, decorated in the style of the mysterious East, with low couches and inlaid Damascus tables, provided guests with other intriguing recreation possibilities. Both ships also featured "a large barber's shop, . . . a clothes-pressing room, a special dining room for maids and valets, a lending library, a telephone system, and a wireless telegraphy installation," *The Shipbuilder* went on. "Indeed everything has been done in regard to the furniture and fittings to make the first-class accommodation more than equal to that provided in the finest hotels on shore."

STYLISH STATEROOMS

Glamorous first-class staterooms on the *Olympic* and *Titanic* were fitted out in a range of styles to suit any expensive taste, including Louis Seize, Empire, Italian Renaissance, Georgian, Regence, Queen Anne, and Old Dutch. The best accommodations aboard each ship were the parlor suites, each consisting of a sitting room, two bedrooms, and two wardrobe rooms, as well as a private bath, lavatory, and, exclusively on the *Titanic,* a private promenade deck. Below: This solid silver lamp from a first-class cabin was recovered from the *Titanic*'s debris field in 1987.

While the *Titanic* was slowly being fitted out, her sister ship, the *Olympic*, set sail with great fanfare and publicity on her maiden voyage to New York on June 14, 1911, leaving Southampton with 1,316 passengers and 850 crew members aboard. Her captain was Edward John (E. J.) Smith, one of the most popular commanders of his day. The white-whiskered commodore, "a splendid seaman" known for his "engaging manner and pleasing personality," had served as skipper of White Star's Majestic for nine years. It had been Smith's honor to take command of many White Star liners on their maiden journeys.

The *Olympic* was acclaimed as "the achievement of the age," the largest and finest product "of the stupendous skill of the first maritime nation of the world." She was so huge that to accommodate her the White Star Line had persuaded the harbor authorities to lengthen New York's Pier 59 by 90 feet into the Hudson River. Although neither she nor the *Titanic* were designed to set speed records, Captain Smith proudly transmitted a wireless dispatch from midocean that the *Olympic* had actually exceeded the speed promised by her builders. Her arrival in New York, attended by twelve tugboats, on June 21, 1911, was greeted with enthusiasm and astonishment at her fantastic size. "She looked to be a genuine sea monster," a New York reporter gawked—so spacious, he enthused, that "It would not be very difficult for two elephants to walk abreast down the main alleyways." Her size and novel recreational attractions even provoked good-natured jabs. A *New York Times* cartoon depicted a well-dressed passenger asking directions to the *Olympic*'s fictitious onboard racetrack. "Walk up two blocks," a deckhand said, "take a red car and—on second thought," he reconsidered, "take the subway."

The *Olympic*'s maiden voyage was an unqualified success. One passenger, however, confessed to having worried about crossing the treacherous Atlantic on the untested liner. On any untried ship, no matter how grand, he noted, "there is always that feeling of an added element of chance. What if this man or that has erred in his estimate, what if the unexpected should happen for just once, what if a dozen different *ifs* should develop to upset the calculations and bring you face to face with the hitherto unencountered?"

But those fears, it turned out, had been totally unfounded. The *Olympic* was safe, secure, triumphantly at port.

"OLYMPIC." FIRST CLASS READING AND WRITING ROOM.

▲ A Georgian-style reading and writing room (above and right) was provided for the comfort of first-class ladies aboard the *Olympic* and *Titanic*.
Above: A pair of reading glasses, belonging to a passenger or crew member, was found near the *Titanic*'s wreck in 1987.

"OLYMPIC." FIRST CLASS DECK "D" DINING SALOON.

▲

The first-class dining room (above and top) seated passengers in luxury and comfort. Second-class accommodations were so well appointed that they equalled or exceeded the first-class facilities aboard other modern ships. Right: A 1920s photo shows passengers enjoying the second-class *Olympic* dining saloon, paneled in the Early English style. On the *Olympic* and *Titanic*, third-class passengers had better accommodations than first-class passengers had enjoyed in earlier days of transatlantic travel.

Both the *Olympic* and *Titanic* featured a popular Verandah Café and Palm Court. Only the *Titanic*, however, offered passengers the Café Parisienne, a trellised replica of a French sidewalk café. Left: Rubberized floor tiles, recovered in 1993, were used in a number of second- and third-class areas. Following spread: A rendering of the Café Parisienne.

"OLYMPIC." FIRST CLASS VERANDAH CAFE AND PALM COURT.

THE MAIDEN VOYAGE

One of the *Titanic*'s great triple-toned whistles, the largest ever built, was retrieved from the wreck site in 1993. Left: The *Titanic* steaming out of Belfast Lough on her sea trials.

NEARLY TEN MONTHS AFTER the *Olympic*'s grand debut, the *Titanic* was at last ready to set sail on her own maiden voyage to New York. The great *Titanic* was everything that the *Olympic* was, and more. She was larger than the first ship by a thousand tons and featured refinements that made her even more splendid than her sister. Many of her opulent new cabins, including twenty-eight extra staterooms on B deck, were graced with real windows instead of portholes, and two had the added luxury of private decks. Thanks in part to the *Olympic*'s great success, White Star had become the transatlantic line preferred by millionaires, transporting more first-class passengers in 1911 than any steamship line in history. To cater to its gilt-edged clientele, White Star added subtle touches that further elevated the *Titanic* above her rivals. The forward end of the great ship's promenade was enclosed with glass to eliminate the annoying seaspray that occasionally splashed the *Olympic*'s first-class strollers. The *Titanic*'s restaurant was larger than the *Olympic*'s and included the tantalizing addition of a Café Parisien, a charming trellised replica of a French sidewalk café. In every way, from her "millionaire suites" to her special accommodations for first-class dogs, the new ship was built to satisfy the craving, particularly of rich Americans, for unbridled luxury in travel. The *Titanic* was similar to the *Olympic*, "but so much more elaborate," explained one of the ship's bakers, Charles Burgess. "Take the dining saloon—*Olympic* didn't even have a carpet, but the *Titanic*—ah, you sank in it up to your knees. Then there's the furniture. So heavy you could hardly lift it. And that panelling . . . it was the care and effort that went into her. She was a beautiful wonderful ship."

On the morning of April 2, 1912, the *Titanic*, the largest ship the world had ever seen, steamed out of Belfast on her sea trials. In the Belfast Lough and the open waters of the Irish Sea, her crew put her through her paces, adjusting her compasses and testing her speed, handling, stopping, starting, and maneuvering abilities. Like her sister ship, the *Titanic* was placed under the experienced command of Captain E. J. Smith. The famous commodore had been transferred from the *Olympic* to take charge of

the *Titanic* on her first Atlantic crossing. The voyage was to be the sixty-two-year-old master's very last command before retiring from his distinguished twenty-six-year career with the White Star Line. Smith was so beloved by wealthy first-class passengers that he was known as the "Millionaire's Captain," and he was equally popular with the crew—"a great favorite, and a man any officer would give his ears to sail under," commented Officer Charles Lightoller, who served with him on the *Titanic*. The highest paid captain afloat, Smith had logged 2 million miles aboard White Star ships and had immense pride in the technology that could produce liners as splendid as the *Olympic* and *Titanic*. "I cannot imagine any condition which would cause a ship to founder. . . . Modern ship-building has gone beyond that," Smith stated definitively in 1907. The master was equally prideful of his record of safe crossings. "When anyone asks me," he said, "how I can best describe my experiences of nearly forty years at sea, I merely say uneventful. I have never been in an accident of any sort worth speaking about. . . . I never saw a wreck and have never been wrecked, nor was I ever in any predicament that threatened to end in disaster of any sort."

Despite that boast, however, Smith's safety record had, in fact, been marred by an 1899 incident, when a White Star liner under his command, the *Germanic*, capsized in New York Harbor as a result of heavy icing. Other distressing situations had more recently occurred when

▲
Captain E. J. Smith, known as the "Millionaire's Captain," commanded the *Titanic* on her maiden voyage. It was to have been the popular captain's last commission before his planned retirement. Above: These brass buttons worn on the uniforms of White Star officers were recovered from the *Titanic's* debris field. Right: The *Titanic* in Southampton on April 10, 1912.

▲

Passengers crowded the White Star Dock at Queenstown, (now Cobh), Ireland, the liner's last stop before steaming into the open Atlantic. Shipping lines competed vigorously to capture the profitable trade of first-class passengers as well as the millions of emigrants who were heading to America.

the *Olympic* was under his command. In June 1911, Smith had damaged a tugboat while guiding the *Olympic* into her New York berth on her maiden voyage. And a few months later, on September 20, 1911, a harrowing accident occurred when the *Olympic* was departing for New York with sixty American millionaires aboard, including Waldorf Astor. The huge liner was leaving Southampton under Smith's command when it suddenly collided with the 7,350-ton Royal Navy cruiser *Hawke*, nearly capsizing the smaller vessel and crumpling its bow like a tin can. Although fortunately no passengers were injured, the impact gored the *Olympic* in two places, ripping a 40-foot-high gash in her starboard side that penetrated 8 feet into her hull. Remarkably, however, there was no panic among the *Olympic*'s genteel passengers; cool and unflappable, they nearly all sat down for luncheon when stewards rang the gong just ten minutes after the collision. It was quite clear, however, that the *Olympic* could

▲

Emigrants at Queenstown waiting to board the *Titanic*. All third-class passengers were required to be examined by a doctor before boarding. Left: This White Star Line second-class luggage tag, indicating a voyage from Southampton to New York, was recovered from the *Titanic*'s wreck site in 1993.

not continue to New York. The gaping hole caused her to list badly to starboard, and she was forced to return to Belfast for six weeks of repairs. Although a Court of Inquiry later faulted the *Olympic* for the accident, Smith's passengers and employers remained unflinchingly loyal to the esteemed commander. "E. J. never took a risk," attested the Bishop of Willesden. "He was a man in whom we had entire and absolute confidence," White Star's Bruce Ismay later pointedly declared.

* * *

ON THE EVENING of April 2, having successfully completed her sea trials, the *Titanic* set course for the port of Southampton. Near midnight on April 3, the great ship gently pulled up at the vast, new 16-acre White Star Dock, constructed especially for the *Titanic* and *Olympic*. The new liner's arrival was a cause for celebration in Southampton—not just because the gargantuan ship was anticipated to be "the last word in ocean travel," but because she brought with her the promise of employment for increasingly desperate Southampton men. The town had been suffering severely from the effects of a six-week national coal miners strike, the largest in the nation's history. With no fuel for their coal-hungry ships, the transatlantic lines had idled their vessels and were

hiring no dockworkers or crews. More than seventeen thousand local men were out of work, and their families were hungry. Despite the strike, however, White Star was determined to maintain its announced schedule for the *Olympic* and *Titanic*. On April 3, the same day that the *Titanic* was tied up at her berth, the *Olympic* sailed out of Southampton as planned, her third-class dining saloon crammed with coal to ensure that she would have enough to fuel her voyage. The *Titanic*, it was announced, would also depart on her maiden crossing as scheduled, at noon on Wednesday, April 10. Although the bitter labor dispute was finally settled on April 6, fresh coal was not yet available in time to fuel the *Titanic* for her departure. To fill her giant bunkers, she was loaded with 4,427 tons of coal scavenged from other I.M.M.-owned ships— the *Oceanic, Majestic, Philadelphia, St. Louis, St. Paul*, and *New York*— whose scheduled crossings had been canceled. Officers and crew were taken on from the other ships as well—and some passengers who had planned to cross aboard the *New York, Philadelphia, Oceanic*, and *Adriatic* found that their bookings had suddenly been changed to the *Titanic*.

* * *

AS THE NEW WHITE STAR leviathan rested in her berth, she seemed truly to be a "Wondership."

More than a sixth of a mile long, the towering *Titanic* loomed over the water like the side of a vast cliff, eleven stories high. Other crafts in the harbor seemed like mere cockleshells beside her, according to an American passenger, Charlotte Collyer. Sightseers streamed into Southampton to see the giant, and some were left practically speechless by her size. The *Titanic*, enthused one tourist, "was huge, I was very overawed, it was magnificent." Her scale was even frightening; "It's *too* big," a Cornishwoman judged. On the other side of the Atlantic, newspapers in New York crowed over the behemoth's eagerly expected arrival on April 17. "When the *Titanic* steams into the Hudson . . . ," proclaimed the *New York Times*, "New Yorkers will see a ship that is more than four city blocks long and which, if stood on end, would be 181.7 feet higher than the Metropolitan Life tower and 270 feet higher than the Singer Building. . . . As for the passenger accommodations, they are among the most gorgeous of any ship ever built."

In safety, too, it was believed, the *Titanic* was the ultimate achievement. "None of us had the slightest fear for her safety," remembered one visitor who toured the ship in Southampton; "she was the last word in modern efficiency and was

▲

The illustration at left shows a first-class bath. Above: This porcelain sink and faucet hardware, simliar to those in the illustration, were recovered from the sea bottom.

said to be literally unsinkable." The *Titanic* was equipped with sixteen watertight compartments, designed so that the ship would float safely even if the two largest sections were flooded with water—an exceedingly unlikely event. Electrically controlled, watertight doors separated the compartments, which could be instantly closed from the captain's bridge. The journal *Engineering* lavished praise on the liner's state-of-the-art safety features. "The *Titanic* . . . embodied all that judgement and knowledge could devise to make her immune from all disaster." With her invincible watertight design, her sixteen wooden lifeboats were considered mere anachronisms, concessions to the skittishness of the traveling public. The *Titanic*'s original plans had called for sixty-four wooden lifeboats. That number had later been cut in half to thirty-two, and by the time the *Titanic* left the shipyard, only sixteen lifeboats had actually been installed, a mere quarter of the original number. Even so, sixteen boats were quite enough to satisfy the archaic Board of Trade regulations. With the addition of four collapsible lifeboats, the *Titanic* had enough lifesaving capacity for 1,178 people—less than half the 3,547 passengers and

crew she was designed to carry. Nevertheless, despite the enormous shortfall, she exceeded existing lifeboat requirements by over 17 percent.

Most of the more than nine hundred crew members who signed aboard the *Titanic* had few qualms about her safety. The *Titanic* was a cut above, "a fine ship . . . much better than the *Olympic*," observed the captain's steward, James Arthur Paintin. Many of the workers were grateful Southampton seamen, and others joined on from Belfast, London, and Liverpool. The vast ship's roster resembled a luxury hotel's, with ranks of carpenters, bakers, icemen, scullions, plate stewards, bedroom stewards, lift attendants, clothes pressers, barbers, and linen keepers in addition to navigating officers, Quartermasters, and stokers. Twenty-three female crew members signed on, too, among them eighteen stewardesses, two cashiers, a third-class matron, a masseuse, and a Turkish bath attendant. There were a number of "special" employees as well. These included the ship's two wireless operators, John G. Phillips and Harold Bride, who were technically employed by the Marconi company but received their paychecks from the White Star Line. Other

HANDS ACROSS THE SEA.

WOVEN IN SILK

R.M.S. TITANIC.

▲

First-class passengers stroll the *Titanic*'s deck. Top: This elegant, silk-paneled postcard from the *Titanic* was posted from Queenstown, Ireland. Previous spread: The stately *Titanic*, "Queen of the Seas," on her maiden voyage.

First-class passenger Frederic O. Spedden watched his six-year-old son, Robert Douglas, play with his top on the promenade deck. Both would survive the disaster. Left: This deck chair from the *Titanic* was found floating in the sea after the sinking. Following spread: An artist's rendering of the *Titanic*'s second-class promenade deck.

special staff members included the restaurant's French and Italian chefs and waiters, who were employed by London restaurateur Luigi Gatti, and the eight members of the ship's band. As a Royal Mail Ship, the *Titanic* also carried five postal clerks: three Americans—Oscar S. Woody, John Starr March, and William Logan Gwinn—and two Englishmen from the Southampton Post Office, John Richard Jago Smith and James Bertram Williamson.

As the April 10 departure date drew closer, the *Titanic*'s last-minute preparations reached a fever pitch. The ship was loaded with vast stores of provisions, crystal, and tableware. Freight was carted aboard, too—most likely not, as some later believed, a fortune in gold and treasure, but less than half a million dollars' worth of ordinary items, such as books, drug sundries, wines, linoleum, sponges, surgical instruments, pamphlets, scientific equipment, window frames, ostrich feathers, and tea. Much of the *Titanic*'s cargo—including laces, silks, and Manchester cotton—was destined for New York retail spring displays of European fashions. As time ran short, workers rushed to apply finishing touches—dangling from the immense funnels to make them sparkle with a last coat of buff-colored paint and frantically struggling to finish carpeting, furnishing, and decorating the huge vessel in time for her sailing date. Work was frustratingly behind

▲

Thomas Andrews, Harland and Wolff's managing director, supervised the *Titanic*'s design and every detail of her construction. He was aboard the vessel making notes late into her last night on potential refinements to the ship. The *Titanic*, Andrews once remarked, was "as nearly perfect as human brains can make her." He did not survive.

schedule, and the pace on the *Titanic* was unusually harsh. "Putting a new ship in commission," Officer Lightoller reflected, "is, at the best of times, a pretty strenuous job." But on the *Titanic*, he noted, "it was night and day work, organizing here, receiving stores there, arranging duties, trying and testing out the different contrivances." Supervising all of the frenzied activity was the *Titanic*'s designer, Thomas Andrews. No detail, no matter how small, escaped his meticulous attention as he endlessly conferred with engineers, officials, and subcontractors, discussed plans, toured the owners around the ship, busied himself adjusting racks, tables, chairs, berth ladders, and electric fans, and oversaw every aspect of the great ship's final completion.

At long last sailing day arrived, and, Lightoller recounted, "from end to end the ship which for days had been like a nest of bees, now resembled a hive about to swarm." Soon after dawn, crew members began to come aboard, changed into their uniforms, and performed a perfunctory thirty-minute boat drill: eighteen men were lowered in two of the ship's lifeboats and "rowed around a couple of turns," Officer Harold Lowe recalled. Shortly afterward, the *Titanic*'s passengers began to stream into the White Star Dock. At 9:30 in the morning, the boat train from Waterloo Station in London arrived in Southampton, discharging many of the

LUXURY ON BOARD THE TITANIC

The *Titanic*'s wealthy passengers included Lady Duff Gordon (right), better known as the couturiere "Madame Lucile," and her husband, Sir Cosmo Duff Gordon. The couple were traveling first-class under the name of "Mr. and Mrs. Morgan" and boarded the *Titanic* at Cherbourg, France, the liner's first stop after leaving Southampton. Both survived the sinking. From their sumptuous cabins to their elegant dinnerware and magnificently appointed public rooms, the *Titanic*'s first-class passengers were pampered in unparalled shipboard style. From left: A first-class silver chocolate pot, emblazoned with the White Star logo, recovered in 1996 (its deformations may have been caused by water pressure after the *Titanic* sank); gilded Spode dinnerware, recovered in 1993 and most likely used in the first-class á la carte restaurant; a bottle of champagne, recovered with its cork intact in 1996 (although sea water had tainted its contents); and the logo of Royal Crown Derby, which manufactured much of the White Star Line's china.

ship's 271 second-class and 712 third-class passengers. Stepping off onto the platform was sixteen-year-old Edith Brown, her father, Thomas, and her mother, Elizabeth. The family had traveled from South Africa and was boarding the *Titanic* en route to starting a new life in Seattle. Other second-class passengers traveling to the White Star Dock that day were a Frenchman named "M. Hoffman," with his two dark-eyed little sons, Michel and Edmond, and Lawrence Beesley, a science teacher from Dulwich who was making his first trip outside England to study American education. Among the passengers transferred to the *Titanic* from other liners were the Harts: seven-year-old Eva, her father, Benjamin, and her mother, Esther. Although Mr. Hart was excited about the switch to the grand new ship, his wife for some reason was desperately unhappy about the prospect of crossing on the *Titanic*. It was the first time in her life, Eva recalled, that she had ever seen her mother crying: "She had this premonition, a most unusual thing for her." Mrs. Hart's dread of the *Titanic* was so great that she refused to go to bed at night aboard the ship. Although a number of others were also anxious about crossing the Atlantic on the *Titanic*'s maiden voyage, most were reassured by her impressive reputation for safety. "God himself

could not sink this ship," proclaimed one deckhand to a nervous second-class passenger.

The third-class travelers who assembled at the White Star Dock came from all over the world. Their profusion of languages—English, French, Polish, Dutch, Russian, Chinese, Swedish, Norwegian, Italian, and Syrian—added to the pandemonium as stewards pointed them along the *Titanic*'s vast labyrinth of corridors and stairways to their accommodations. Finding his way among the steerage crowds was a young American named Henry Sutehall, Jr. The twenty-six-year-old was returning home to Kenmore, New York, after an extended round-the-world trip in the company of his good friend Howard Irwin. The two young men, who by trade were trimmers of coach and automobile interiors, had traveled west from New York State with just fifty dollars and a violin. Somehow, with good fortune and a world's worth of experiences, they had made their way from Buffalo to Cleveland, Chicago, St. Louis, Denver, Salt Lake City, San Francisco, Los Angeles,

▲
The *Olympic* and *Titanic* were among the first ocean liners to feature swimming baths, deep, marble-tiled pools filled with salt water. Right: This telephone, found at the *Titanic*'s wreck site in 1987, was probably used for communicating from the after docking bridge to the engine room or navigation bridge.

Seattle, and Portland, then on to Australia, the Suez, and Europe. Now Sutehall was returning home on the *Titanic*. Mysteriously, however, Irwin himself was not booked as a passenger on the *Titanic*'s maiden voyage.

At 11:30 in the morning, many of the *Titanic*'s wealthiest passengers pulled up at the dock on the special first-class boat train from London, ornamented with rich blue upholstery and gold braid. Among the noteworthy arrivals, many accompanied by personal valets, maids, and other servants, was W. T. Stead, who was regarded as the most brilliant journalist in England. The white-bearded social critic was the influential editor of the *Review of Reviews* and the *Pall Mall Gazette*; he was traveling to New York at the personal request of President Taft, who had invited him to give a speech at the World Peace Conference at Carnegie Hall on April 21.

Another distinguished first-class passenger was Major Archibald Butt, Taft's popular forty-one-year-old military aide and close personal adviser. Butt had enjoyed multiple careers as soldier, journalist, diplomat, and novelist. Lately, however, he had been feeling exceedingly fatigued and stressed. Persuaded that a trip might do him good, he had traveled to Rome to meet with the pope and King Victor Emmanuel on behalf of the U.S. President. He was now returning home on the *Titanic* in the company of his good friend, the famous artist and former war correspondent Francis D. Millet. Colonel Archibald Gracie, an amateur military historian who had just published his book *The Truth about Chickamauga*, had traveled abroad to refresh himself and research his next book and was looking forward to a relaxing voyage home.

Millionaires had booked passage on the *Titanic*, too. Isidor Straus, an owner of Macy's department store and a former member of Congress, was returning home to New York with his wife, Ida, after spending a winter holiday on the French Riviera. George Widener, scion of the richest family in Philadelphia, boarded the *Titanic* with his wife and twenty-seven-year-old son Harry. The wealthiest passenger on the luxurious new ship was Colonel John Jacob Astor. The builder and owner of more hotels and skyscrapers than any other New Yorker, Astor had a personal fortune estimated at $100 million. Money, however, had not been enough to purchase his acceptance in the most sought-after social circles. New York and Newport society had bitterly opposed Astor's divorce in 1909 and his remarriage two years later to a scandalously young woman, the eighteen-year-old Madeleine Force. Ostracised by social arbiters, the couple had fled New York for a tour of Egypt and Paris. Astor and his young wife, who was five months pregnant, were now returning home, hoping to reenter society after their extended trip.

▲

Colonel John Jacob Astor was the wealthiest passenger on the *Titanic* with a fortune estimated at $100 million. After a long holiday abroad, he was returning home with his young wife, Madeleine, who was five months pregnant. She survived the sinking but he did not.

Before the *Titanic*'s scheduled noon departure, passengers, reporters, and visitors wandered all over the ship—riding the electric lifts, inspecting the purser's office and the kitchens with their remarkable time-saving contraptions, exploring the libraries and other public rooms, peering into the squash court, and amusing themselves on the gymnasium's mechanical equipment. All the while, the ship's band, directed by thirty-three-year-old violinist Wallace Hartley, regaled the crowd on deck with lively ragtime and operetta tunes. Then, promptly at noon, the *Titanic*'s immense, triple-toned steam whistle pierced the air three times, visitors debarked, and the great liner majestically got underway, assisted by the tugboats *Hector*, *Hercules*, *Neptune*, *Ajax*, *Albert Edward*, and *Vulcan*. The crowds thronging the docks cheered, handkerchiefs fluttered in the breeze, and passengers tossed flowers into the water as the *Titanic* slowly left her berth and steamed into the River Test at a stately speed of about 6 knots. The sight of the magnificent *Titanic* left an indelible impression on many in the crowd that lined the shore. "She looked colossal and so queenly," a reporter wrote, as passengers waved spirited good-byes from her decks and windows.

Instantly, however, the great ship's maiden voyage headed for disaster. The immense *Titanic* had displaced so much water that her wake had busted the stout moorings of the berthed liner *New York*. The thick ropes snapped with a report like gunshots and flung themselves perilously into the dockside crowd. A 6-foot gangway crashed into the water, and the untethered *New York* rammed straight ahead for the *Titanic*. It was only fast maneuvering by the harbor pilot, George Bowyer, and Captain Smith that averted a terrifying collision. "It was a narrow squeak," noted Captain Gale, whose tugboat *Vulcan* finally caught hold of the *New York* "like a naughty child." It seemed an inauspicious start to some aboard. "That's a bad omen," second-class

The *Titanic* left Southampton on her maiden voyage shortly after midday on April 10, 1912 (opposite page). Above: Minutes after leaving her berth, the *Titanic* narrowly escaped a collision with the liner *New York*, whose moorings had snapped from the *Titanic*'s enormous wake. Right: In this letter, posted from Queenstown, first-class passenger Hugh Woolner described the near disaster. Following spread: A rendering of a first-class stateroom as it may have appeared in 1912.

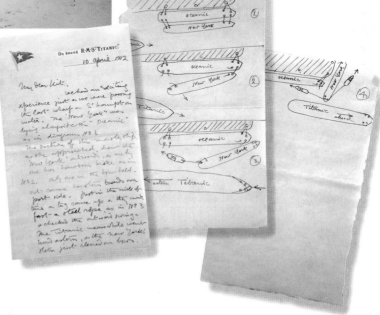

▲

On the *Titanic*, men enjoyed the
sanctum of a sumptuous,
Georgian-style first-class smoking
room similar to this one on the
Olympic (above and left)—"the
finest apartment of its kind"—
paneled in mahogany with mother-
of-pearl inlays. Top: Cigarettes
and a pipe recovered from the
Titanic's wreck site in 1987.

passenger Thomas Brown grimly remarked to his daughter, Edith. One crew member, Able Seaman Joseph Scarrett, was so shaken by the near miss that he was ready to abandon the ship: "I said to a chum of mine 'I am going to get my bag and if the *New York* drops alongside I'm going . . . ,'" he declared.

For most, however, the close call was soon forgotten in the enchantment of the first hours at sea. It was a bright spring afternoon, and as the great ship headed out of Southampton Water, passengers were quickly summoned to their first meal by the cheery bugling of "The Roast Beef of Old England." The afternoon passed comfortably as the majestic liner gently crossed the open waters of the English Channel, arriving at her first port in Cherbourg, France, at 6:35 in the evening. As the sun set, the *Titanic* rested in Cherbourg's deep-water harbor, taking aboard mail and 274 additional passengers who were ferried out by tenders. The 142 new

first-class arrivals included wealthy Americans heading to New York after spending the social season in Europe. Among them were Mrs. Charlotte Drake Cardeza, who came aboard with fourteen trunks, four suitcases, and three crates of baggage; Charles Melville Hays, president of the Canadian Grand Trunk Railroad; John B. Thayer, president of the Pennsylvania Railroad; and American millionairess Mrs. James Joseph ("Molly") Brown of Denver. The estranged wife of a newly minted millionaire from Leadville, Colorado, Mrs. Brown had befriended the Astors in Egypt and had booked passage on the *Titanic* in order to accompany them on the crossing to New York. Benjamin Guggenheim, the American mining and smelting magnate, had originally booked a cabin on the *Lusitania* but transferred to the *Titanic* at Cherbourg when the Cunard ship was idled for repairs.

Thirty second-class passengers also came aboard, including Franz Pulbaum, a twenty-seven-year-old machinist from Germany. Pulbaum had emigrated to the United States at the age of twenty-two and had evidently done quite well in his new home. After traveling to Europe, he was returning to his adopted country in grand style, on the poshest, most fabled ship in the world. More than a hundred steerage passengers boarded at Cherbourg, too, many of them emigrants from Syria

This document, the property of second-class passenger Franz Pulbaum, was also recovered from the ocean bottom. It declared the twenty-seven-year-old German emigrant's intent to become a citizen of the United States. Left: Denver millionairess Mrs. James Joseph Brown, popularly remembered as "the unsinkable Molly Brown." Left: A sapphire and diamond ring, belonging to one of the *Titanic*'s passengers, was found near the wreck in 1987.

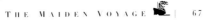

▲

First-class passengers on the *Titanic* and *Olympic* had the convenience of three electric elevators. Second-class passengers—for the first time on any transatlantic liner—had the luxury of an elevator as well. Left: A bow tie recovered from the *Titanic's* debris field.

▲

Decorations in the first-class
lounge aboard the *Olympic* and
Titanic (above and left) were mod-
eled on the Palace of Versailles.
Top: A chandelier from one of the
Titanic's first-class public rooms.

A PASSENGER'S BELONGINGS

Among the *Titanic*'s third-class passengers was an American carriage and automobile tradesman named Henry Sutehall, Jr. Sutehall and his good friend Howard Irwin were originally from Buffalo, New York, and had been traveling around the world together, earning money by working occasionally as day laborers. Sutehall was listed as a passenger on the *Titanic* and was evidently returning home after his extended journey. Irwin, however, does not appear on the *Titanic*'s passenger list; perhaps he was not aboard the ship or was traveling under an assumed name, a relatively common practice in the early twentieth century. In 1993, a wooden trunk containing many of Irwin's personal possessions was recovered from the bottom of the North Atlantic. Many of his papers, including letters and sheet music, were in remarkably good condition because they had been packed in a cloth bag inside the trunk. The discoveries included (clockwise beginning at right): a copy of the *Coachmakers' Journal,* an industry publication from New South Wales, Australia, where Irwin and Sutehall may have sought work in their trade; the wooden handle of a leather trimming tool; a music stand made to be attached to a clarinet; sheet music for a popular tune of the day; a clarinet; a leather belt decorated with floral embossing; and a North Buffalo Lodge membership list in which Howard Irwin's name is seen. Irwin's friend Henry Sutehall, Jr., did not survive the voyage home.

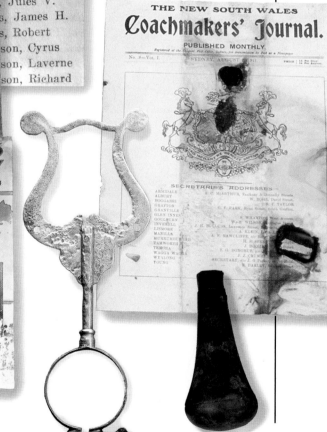

The *Titanic*'s first-class lounge was
a social gathering place for many
wealthy passengers.

and Croatia. And twenty-two passengers ended their *Titanic* voyage in France, including eleven-year-old Eileen Lenox-Conyngham, who was headed on holiday with her mother, her Aunt Alice, and her ten-year-old brother, Denis. The four had chosen to cross the Channel aboard the *Titanic* because they "wanted the largest, safest, steadiest ship afloat."

As darkness slowly settled on the French coast, the *Titanic*, magnificently lit from bow to stern, gleamed like a floating city on the sea. "Her outline was etched clearly in light," an observer recalled, "with each porthole gleaming like a star." The magnificent *Titanic*, queen of the seas, glided gracefully out of Cherbourg Harbor at ten past eight, her great mass riding steady on the ocean swells. Cocooned in incomparable luxury and comfort, passengers chatted and renewed acquaintances, enjoyed an orchestra concert, and settled in for their first evening at sea, lulled by the calm stability of the world's largest, grandest ship. In the morning, on Thursday, April 11, they sighted land again, as the *Titanic* made her last call at the port of Queenstown (now Cobh) on the rugged Irish coast. Anchored some two miles offshore, the *Titanic* took on another 7 second-class passengers, 113 third-class passengers, and 194 sacks of mail. A few travelers got off the ship at Queenstown—including a twenty-four-year-old fireman, John Coffey, who smuggled himself

▲
Second-class passengers gaze out over the deck of the *Titanic*. Left: 120 second- and third-class passengers and 194 sacks of mail were brought aboard the *Titanic* at Queenstown. Besides mail, the ship was carrying one motor car crated as cargo.

ashore under a pile of empty mail bags. "I still don't like this ship. . . . I have a queer feeling about it," wrote Chief Officer Wilde in a letter posted to his sister from the Irish port.

To journalist W. T. Stead and most other passengers aboard, however, there was nothing the least bit sinister about the *Titanic*. She was a pleasure palace, "a monstrous floating Babylon" filled with delights. At 1:30 on the afternoon of April 11, with 1,321 passengers and 908 crew members aboard, the massive ship's great whistles intoned again three times, and the leviathan steamed out for the open sea. The blue-green ocean was calm, and on the morning after leaving Queenstown, science teacher Beesley wrote, "the sun rose behind us in a sky of circular clouds. . . . It was a beautiful sight to one who had not crossed the ocean before. . . . " There couldn't be a smoother, more delightful maiden voyage. Passengers whiled away the hours reading, writing letters, and strolling on the decks. Others played hands of bridge or poker, listened to orchestra concerts, or enjoyed coffee at the Café Parisien. "I enjoyed myself," Colonel Gracie wrote, "as if I were in a summer palace on the seashore, surrounded with every comfort—there was nothing to indicate or suggest that we were on the stormy Atlantic Ocean." The sea was so calm that most were even able to indulge in the luxuriously rich meals that were served in the first- and second-class saloons. Third-class passengers ate heartily, too—as well, it was said, as first-class passengers on older ships. Many played ball games on deck and danced to the music of an Irish pipe and fiddle or the piano that was provided for their entertainment. Quite a few of the steerage passengers, in fact, were at leisure, in comfortable surroundings, for the first time in their lives. The ocean was like a millpond, journalist Stead wrote to his wife, the weather was fine and cool, and the *Titanic* was a floating pleasure garden, "as firm as a rock" in the sea.

All was not so quiet and serene, how-ever, belowdecks. A fire had been smoldering steadily in one of the *Titanic*'s coal bunkers ever since the liner had left Belfast. And on Friday evening at eleven o'clock, the ship's wireless system unaccountably broke down. The Marconi operators, Phillips and Bride, finally fixed the circuit problem by five on Saturday morning, and by noon, recalled Lead Fireman Fred Barrett, the coal fire was at last put out. No more dangers appeared to threaten the invincible *Titanic*. There was nothing further out of the ordinary to concern the captain or the crew, save for the wireless warnings of ice that the *Titanic* had been receiv-

▲

This chocolate pot and vermeil sauce boat were used to serve the *Titanic*'s first-class passengers. Both were recovered from the wreck site in 1987.

ing from other ships in the North Atlantic lanes. On Thursday, several ice warnings had been posted in the *Titanic*'s chart room. On Friday, the French steamship *La Touraine* had telegraphed that she had passed through "a thick ice field." And on Saturday, the steamer *Rappahannock* alerted the *Titanic* that she, too, had encountered a massive field of ice. April was known to be one of the most dangerous months for ice, but bergs in huge numbers were drifting further south than they had in fifty years, jamming the North Atlantic lanes. Many vessels, including the Cunard liner *Carmania*, had reported being shut in by dense fields of low-lying ice "growlers" on every side of the horizon.

Despite these ice alerts, however, the *Titanic* raced across the vast and calm Atlantic. Each day on the quiet sea after leaving Queenstown, Captain Smith gradually unleashed the power of the *Titanic*'s great engines, proudly noting her increasing speed as she steamed 386 miles on Friday, April 12, 519 miles on Saturday, April 13, and 546 miles on Sunday, April 14. Three days later, on Wednesday, April 17, she would glide proudly into New York Harbor. The engines churned, and the great ship steamed steadily ahead.

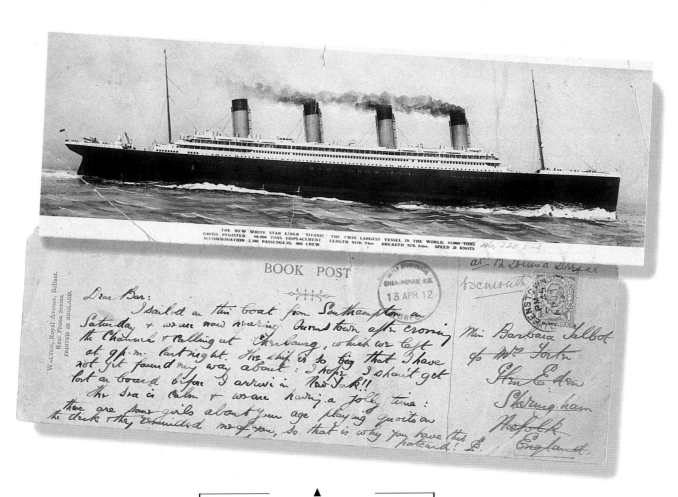

This extra-large postcard, almost a foot
long, was a novelty in its day. The card was
mailed from the *Titanic* and postmarked at
Queenstown, Ireland, on April 13, 1912.
Following spread: The *Titanic* steams off into
the sunset on April 14, 1912.

TERROR AT SEA

A pair of opera or field glasses found near the *Titanic*'s wreck. Left: Many ships reported that the North Atlantic shipping lanes were jammed with floating icefields in April 1912.

THE SEA WAS SMOOTH as glass on Sunday, April 14, the *Titanic*'s fourth day out at sea. In the clear, cool morning, strollers paced the deck, braving the chill wind before breakfast. Others began the day in the warm comfort of the great ship's public rooms or drifted into the gymnasium, lured by instructor T. W. McCawley, crisply dressed as usual in his impeccable white flannels. A bit later, at 10:30 in the morning, passengers from all classes gathered in the first-class dining room for Divine Services. Captain Smith himself led the shipboard congregation, reading from the White Star Line's own prayer book, while a five-man orchestra directed by Wallace Hartley accompanied the hymns. Although Sunday services were customarily followed by a lifeboat drill for passengers and crew, Captain Smith elected to forego this formality on the *Titanic*'s first calm Sabbath day at sea. Instead, passengers relaxed before sitting down to an elaborate luncheon. For many, the voyage had settled into a sublime routine, an endless round of dinner parties, bridge parties, dancing, auction pools, and rich repasts. "The days passed too quickly," recalled first-class passenger Mrs. René Harris. "I felt as if I would like to go on until the end of time."

Things were not so luxuriously paced, however, in the *Titanic*'s wireless room. The ship's Marconi operators, John Phillips and his assistant Harold Bride, were hectically receiving and transmitting private telegrams across the ocean for the *Titanic*'s wealthy passengers—including a substantial backlog of personal messages that had piled up while the wireless had been broken down on Friday night. Whenever the splutter and buzz of Morse code communicated a warning from another ship related to safety or navigation, Phillips and Bride interrupted their personal transmissions and brought the message to the attention of the captain and the ship's officers. They were receiving a number of these navigation alerts on Sunday. At nine o'clock in the morning, the *Caronia* had signaled: "Bergs, growlers and field ice 42° to 51° W." The captain had been given this message on the bridge and had then posted the information for his officers. Shortly before noon, at 11:40 A.M., the *Noordam* radioed the *Titanic* of "Much ice," and at 1:42 P.M., the *Baltic* cautioned: "Icebergs and large quantities of field ice in 41° 51' N, 40° 52' W," a position close to the *Titanic*'s route. This warning, too, was handed to the captain. Smith then passed the message on to his employer, J. Bruce Ismay, who was presiding over the *Titanic* on her maiden voyage. Ismay silently placed the warning in his pocket before going in to luncheon. Later, the White Star chairman casually brought it out to show a number of passengers. "I suppose you are going to slow her down," commented Mrs. Arthur Ryerson to Ismay when he remarked that the *Titanic* was approaching ice. "Oh, no," Ismay replied, she recalled. "On the contrary, we are going to let her run a great deal faster and get out of it." At three minutes past five o'clock, Phillips and Bride

▲

On the *Titanic*'s final day, second-class passenger Lawrence Beesley (above) recalled gazing at his baggage receipt, No. 208. The other half of his receipt, which was kept by the purser, was found at the bottom of the sea in 1987.

intercepted yet another warning from the eastbound liner *Amerika*: "Two icebergs in 41° 27' N, 50° 8' W on April 14."

To most of those on board, the only sign of changing sea conditions was the sudden drop in temperature as the afternoon wore on. By 5:30 P.M., the air had begun to chill rapidly, and passengers abandoned their deck chairs for warmer comforts indoors. Some opted for the attractions of the main lounge, where band-members performed Strauss waltzes and Gilbert and Sullivan melodies. Others relaxed over tea and toast, played hands of patience, and strolled the ship's covered promenades. In the library, Lawrence Beesley passed time by filling out his baggage declaration form, glancing idly at the receipt—No. 208—that the purser had given him for his valuables, an envelope containing cash. Below, in steerage, emigrants whiled away the increasingly bracing afternoon by playing cards in their smoking room and dancing in the third-class general room. Outside, the temperature continued to fall rapidly, plummeting to 33°F by 7:30. By 8:40, the unusual cold had alarmed Second Officer Lightoller; he sent the ship's carpenter to look after the fresh water supply, which he worried was about to freeze.

Before going in to dinner, Captain Smith had tracked down Ismay in the first-class smoking room and asked him to return the *Baltic*'s ice warning so it could be posted in the officer's chart room. Meanwhile, Phillips and Bride were continuing to receive ice alerts. At 7:30, they intercepted a caution

An unidentified wireless operator in a shipboard Marconi telegraph room probably similar to the *Titanic*'s. By 1912, all North Atlantic passenger ships carried wireless equipment. Right: The *Titanic*'s two wireless operators, John Phillips and Harold Bride, were technically employed by the Marconi company but received their paychecks from the White Star Line.

from the nearby *Californian*: "42° 3' N, 49° 9' W. Three large bergs 5 miles to the southward of us." Captain Smith, however, was not informed of this navigation warning, since he was being feted in the restaurant as guest of honor at a dinner party hosted by the Wideners. The mood of everyone in the restaurant, recalled a first-class passenger, "was very gay, and at neighboring tables people were making bets on the probable time of this record-breaking run. . . . Mr. Ismay said that undoubtedly the ship would establish a record." After dinner, Captain Smith lingered over a cigar; other passengers enjoyed coffee in the Palm Court, where the orchestra entertained them with romantic music from *The Tales of Hoffmann*.

As the hours passed, passengers settled down for another quiet evening on the sea. Many prominent first-class men—including Major Butt, Francis Millet, John Thayer, Colonel Gracie, and George Widener—retired to the comfortable smoking room, where they talked politics and traded stories of travel and adventure. In the second-class dining saloon, a hundred passengers gathered to sing religious hymns, led by the Reverend E. C. Carter, and in steerage, small groups of emigrants sat talking about their new country and the new lives they would be starting in only three short days. "All of my companions," remembered third-class passenger Abraham Hyman, "were

The *Titanic*'s prominent passengers included John B. Thayer, second vice-president of the Pennsylvania Railroad (above); Colonel Archibald Gracie (top left); former war correspondent Francis D. Millet (lower left); and George Widener, a member of the richest family in Philadelphia (top right). Facing page: White Star chairman J. Bruce Ismay was also aboard. Only Ismay and Gracie survived.

very glad that the voyage was coming to an end."

The *Titanic*'s designer, Thomas Andrews, however, had spent most of the evening alone in his cabin studying plans of the ship and noting changes that should be made, based on the first four days at sea. No detail had escaped Andrew's notice, from the excessive number of screws in stateroom hat racks to the color of the pebble dashing on the private decks. Earlier in the day, he had confided to a friend that he believed the *Titanic* to be "as nearly perfect as human brains can make her." While the designer continued to focus intently on his notes, seventeen-year-old passenger Jack Thayer, son of the Pennsylvania Railroad vice-president, decided to stretch his legs out on the Boat Deck. Wandering under the stars in the cold mid-Atlantic air, he was struck by the immense beauty of the evening. "It was a brilliant, starry night," he vividly recalled. "There was no moon, and I have never seen the stars shine brighter; they appeared to stand out of the sky, sparkling like diamonds. . . . It was the kind of night that made one feel glad to be alive."

A little before nine o'clock, the captain bade goodnight to his dinner companions and stopped in at the bridge, where he instructed Lightoller to notify him immediately if conditions became hazy. The *Titanic* was speeding across the sea at a brisk pace of 22.5 knots, the fastest she had ever steamed on her maiden crossing. "If it becomes at all doubtful," the captain warned, "let me know at once. I shall be just inside." Aside from the falling temperature, it was a perfect night. There was no wind, remembered Able Seaman Joseph Scarrett; "the sea was as calm as a lake. . . . Everybody was in good spirits, and everything throughout the ship was going smoothly."

By 10:30, however, the sea's temperature had plunged to 31 degrees, and in the bitterly cold rushing air up in the crow's nest, the two lookouts, Frederick Fleet and Reginald Lee, strained their eyes to watch out for ice, as they had been instructed. The best way to see an iceberg from a distance was to spot the ring of white foam made by waves lapping against the base of the exposed ice, a sign clearly visible in wind or swell. Tonight, however, there wasn't a ripple on the water. There was, though, a strange, clammy odor in the air. "By the smell of it," a lookout on the previous shift had guessed, "there is ice about." More ice warnings had, in fact, continued to come in over the wireless throughout the evening. At 9:40 P.M. the *Mesaba* had telegraphed: "Ice reported in latitude 42° 25' N, longitude 49° to 50° 30' W. Saw much heavy pack ice and great number large icebergs; also field ice." Phillips dutifully recorded this message; however, his attention was focused on the volume of private messages he needed to send now that the *Titanic* was in range of the land-based Marconi station at Cape Race. He set the ice warning aside

under a paperweight, intending to deliver it to the bridge when he could spare the time. It was still on his table at eleven o'clock, when a nearby ship, the *Californian*, interrupted Phillips's Morsing to report that she was completely blocked by ice. Annoyed at the radio intrusion, Phillips signaled back, "Shut up. Shut up. I am busy. I am working Cape Race." Rebuffed, the tired Marconi operator on the *Californian* turned off his receiver and went to bed.

* * *

BY 11:40, STEWARDS WERE turning down the lights throughout the *Titanic*'s emptying public rooms, and the last social gatherings were finally breaking up. Most of the passengers had already straggled off to bed. The great ship was calm and silent, from her grand saloons to her empty corridors, as she raced through the brilliant, moonless night. Up in the crow's nest, however, Frederick Fleet was increasingly alarmed by a strange haze he noticed directly ahead on the horizon. He and Lee struggled to make out what lay ahead with their bare eyes; the binoculars that should have been in the crow's nest were for some reason missing. Suddenly, Fleet frantically jerked the warning bell three times and telephoned the bridge, sputtering, "Iceberg, right ahead!" into the mouthpiece. "Thank you," Sixth Officer Moody briskly replied. The *Titanic* was hurtling directly toward a pinnacled black mass of

▲
The ship's boiler and engine rooms were separated by massive watertight doors that were electrically controlled from the bridge. Top: Large bell from the base of the foremast recovered from the *Titanic*'s wreck in 1987. Following page: An illustration published a month after the *Titanic* disaster showed an iceberg ripping a huge gash in the ship, an erroneous but commonly held belief.

ice, and Fleet and Lee steeled themselves for a disastrous collision. But below, First Officer William Murdoch took quick evasive action—ordering the ship's engines stopped, reversed, then turned hard to port—and instantly shut the ship's fifteen watertight doors. The lookouts clung on as the *Titanic*'s prow swerved slowly to port; instead of smashing into the towering berg head on, she scraped against the looming ice for a full ten seconds on her starboard side.

Captain Smith felt the impact and rushed into the chart room. "What have we struck, Mr. Murdoch?" he inquired. "An iceberg, sir," Murdoch replied. "I hard-a-starboarded and reversed the engines and I was going to hard-a-port around it, but she was too close. I could not do any more." The officers quickly sent for Thomas Andrews—who, engrossed in his work, hadn't noticed the collision—and Fourth Officer Boxhall was ordered to make a cursory inspection of the forward areas. Although Boxhall returned with no report of damage, Smith and Andrews decided to reconnoiter for themselves, moving along the ship's companionways to avoid alarming passengers. What the two men saw was horrifying. A spur of ice jutting from the iceberg below the waterline had scraped along the *Titanic*'s underside for 300 feet, damaging the ship's inch-

▲

After the collision, the *Titanic*'s wireless operators, Phillips and Bride, ceaselessly transmitted telegrams pleading for urgent assistance, until all power was lost at 2:17 A.M. Despite their efforts, a nearby ship—the *Californian*—failed to hear the distress calls because its wireless operator was asleep and its Marconi set had been turned off. Phillips, twenty-eight, went down with the ship. Bride, twenty-two, survived.

thick plates in at least five and perhaps six of her watertight compartments. Sea water was now rushing into the ship's first five compartments and had already climbed fourteen feet above the keel—and the *Titanic* was incapable of floating with more than the first four compartments flooded. Although pumps were so far keeping the sea out of boiler room 6, icy water was now bursting in from the forepeak to boiler room 5 as the ship's bow sank under the weight, filling one watertight compartment after another like sections of an ice-cube tray. "How long have we?" Captain Smith asked Thomas Andrews. Harland and Wolff's managing director scribbled some figures on a piece of paper. "An hour and a half," he judged. "Possibly two. Not much longer." The *Titanic*, they knew with terrifying certainty, was doomed. At the captain's request, Boxhall quickly estimated their position and jotted it on a scrap of paper. The commander took the note to the wireless shack and told Phillips to send out the Marconi call for assistance, CQD, followed by the *Titanic*'s call letters, MGY, and the ship's position.

The officers were not the only ones who already knew the graveness of the situation. In boiler room 6, leading stoker Frederick Barrett had been startled by a noise like thunder, followed by a gush of water that surged in through the ship's side just two feet in front of him. As the watertight door between boiler rooms 5 and 6 suddenly began to descend, stoker George Beauchamp and engineer John Henry Hesketh dashed through, and Barrett narrowly climbed to safety up an emergency escape ladder. Just fifteen minutes after the collision, the *Titanic*'s post office was already flooded with two feet of water, and the five postal workers were scrambling to lug two hundred sacks of mail to a dry deck above. As soon as they had finished, however, sea water was already foaming around them, and they struggled with the sacks again, this time up steep staircases to another level.

Other workers, however, were unaware of the danger they were in. Fireman John Podesta had been lying in his bunk when he heard a crash that "sounded like tearing a strip off a piece of calico—nothing more, only a quiver. It did not even wake those who were in a good sleep." Soon, however, Podesta and his mates could hear water rushing into the forward hold, and he began shaking fireman Gus Stanbrook, who was still sleeping in his bunk, saying, "'Come on Gus, get a life belt and go to your boat, she's sinking.' He began laughing and simply lay back again, thinking it was a joke." Seaman Joseph Scarrett had been enjoy-

ing a smoke when the ship started shaking. "Those of the crew who were asleep in their bunks turned out, and we all rushed on deck to see what was the matter. We found the ship had struck an iceberg as there was a large quantity of ice . . . on the starboard side of the foredeck. We did not think it very serious so went below again, cursing the iceberg for disturbing us."

Many of the passengers, too, had no idea that the ship was in great peril. There was "no cry in the night; no alarm given; no one afraid," Beesley recalled. In her cabin, Mrs. J. Stuart White noticed a strange vibration during the collision, as though the ship "went over a thousand marbles." Elizabeth Shutes remembered only bitterly cold air pouring into her stateroom and a strange odor, "as if it came from a clammy cave." Lady Duff Gordon heard a noise that sounded "as though someone had drawn a giant finger all along the side of the boat." Mrs. Hart "felt this little bump. . . . Had she been asleep it wouldn't have wakened her," her daughter, Eva, recalled. Mrs. Hart woke her husband and sent him to question a sailor. He came back, his daughter remembered, and said, "'We've hit an iceberg . . . they're going to launch the lifeboats but you'll all be back on board for breakfast.'"

▲ **S**crews, bolts, and pulleys from a davit that once held *Titanic* lifeboats were recovered from the wreck site in 1993. The *Titanic* carried only sixteen wooden lifeboats, a quarter of the number she had originally been designed to hold. Below: A nameplate from one of the lifeboats that carried survivors from the ship.

Outside, several steerage passengers were entertaining themselves by kicking around the ice that had dropped onto the deck, and some first-class passengers laughingly arranged snowball matches for the next morning. Three French passengers had been playing bridge with a Mr. Smith of Philadelphia when a "crunching mass of ice packed up against the portholes." Immediately after the collision, professional gamblers were gathering up their cards, which had fallen to the floor, and were dealing hands again. In the smoking room, one of the card players pointed to his whiskey glass and jokingly suggested that someone run out on deck for ice to chill his drink.

Some passengers, however, had found the impact terrifying. Martha Stephenson had been sound asleep when she was awakened "by a terrible jar with ripping and cutting noises." She and her sister, Elizabeth Eustis, were frightened, but their steward reassured them, saying, "No, it's only cold, go to bed; it's nothing at all." In the corridors outside, many people were wandering about halfdressed. Some had already begun to talk of lifeboats, but few took the subject seriously. "What do they need of lifeboats?" one woman asked. "This ship could smash a hundred icebergs and not feel it. Ridiculous!" she announced. "Everyone seemed confident that the ship was all right," recalled passenger Henry Sleeper Harper. After being reassured by stewards

that the ship would merely be delayed two hours before steaming on to New York, some passengers even headed back to bed.

Soon, however—despite the fact that no general warning had been issued—the shout came: "All passengers on deck with life belts on." In states of dress and undress, some barefoot or in their stocking feet, passengers obediently fastened bulky life vests over sweeping dinner gowns and motor coats, kimonos, and fur coats hastily thrown over their nightclothes. "It was," remarked Helen Churchill Candee, "a fancy-dress ball in Dante's Hell." Lawrence Beesley wisely put on a warm Norfolk jacket, tied on his life belt, and tucked two books he had been reading into his side pockets; steward James Johnson stuffed four oranges into his shirt. The crowd moved—wordless, orderly, and quiet—up the sweep of the grand stairway. Some lined up at the purser's office to collect their valuables, which the staff distributed with cool efficiency. In steerage, too, passengers remained remarkably calm when officers woke them and told them to come up on deck. Some could clearly tell, however, that things were amiss. "When I started to dress," remembered third-class passenger Carl Jonsson, "I noticed there was water creeping up about my feet. At first it came very slowly, but after a time," he noted, "it was around my ankles."

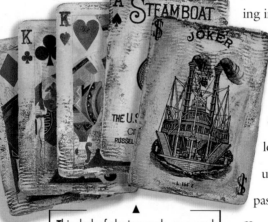

This deck of playing cards, recovered from the sea bottom in 1993, was found in a trunk containing the possessions of Howard Irwin, who may have been a passenger on board. Right: In third class, passenger Carl Jonsson noticed water rising up to his ankles shortly after the collision. He survived.

In this 1912 illustration, titled "Meet Me in New York," a husband kisses his wife good-bye from the *Titanic*'s Boat Deck as women and children board the lifeboats.

DRAWN FROM MATERIAL SUPPLIED BY MR. F. M. HOYT, A SURVIVOR.

THE CHIVALRY OF THE SEA: "WOMEN AND CHILDREN FIRST" AFTER THE "TITANIC" DISASTER.

THE ORDER "ALL MEN STAND BACK AWAY FROM THE BOATS. ALL LADIES RETIRE TO THE NEXT DECK
BELOW": WOMEN ENTERING A LIFE-BOAT FROM B DECK OF THE "TITANIC."

SHORTLY AFTER MIDNIGHT, Captain Smith ordered sailors to make the sixteen lifeboats and four collapsible boats ready—although he was fully aware that there was only enough lifeboat space to evacuate half the passengers and crew members on board. Before leaving Southampton, the crew had never had more than a cursory lifeboat drill; now they worked as best they could to prepare and lower the boats and obey the captain's order. The immense *Titanic* lay strangely still on the water, its quiet broken only by the infernal noise of steam being released to ease the pressure in the boilers. The din was like "twenty locomotives blowing off steam in a low key," and conversation was nearly impossible. Even so, Beesley recalled, "no signs of alarm were exhibited by any one: there was no indication of panic or hysteria; no cries of fear, and no running to and fro to discover what was the matter, why we had been summoned on deck with lifebelts, and what was to be done with us now we were there."

Soon, Lightoller shouted to the captain for permission to load women and children into the boats. Captain Smith nodded his assent, then retreated into the wireless room. Despite the best efforts of the crewmen to get passengers into the lifeboats, however, many women were reluctant to leave their husbands and the foundering ship. After all, Beesley explained, the water "looked a

THE IRISH EMIGRANT (4).

I'm bidding you a long farewell, my Mary kind and true.
But I'll not forget you darling, in the land I'm goin' to ;
They say there's bread and work for all, and the sun shines always there,
But I'll ne'er forget " Ould Ireland " were it fifty times as fair, were it fifty times as fair.

On the back of this postcard, mailed from Queenstown, an emigrant wrote to his beloved: "I am sailing today, Thursday on *Titanic* on her maiden trip to New York, her first trip on the Atlantic. Good bye. Love, Patrick Dooley." Dooley perished in the disaster. An eyewitness account by a survivor, Mr. F. M. Hoyt, inspired the illustration at left of women and children descending in a lifeboat. Bottom left: This life jacket, worn by a victim of the disaster, was retrieved by the crew of the *Mackay-Bennett*, a cable ship sent to recover bodies from the sea in the days after the sinking.

tremendous way down in the darkness, the sea and the night both seemed very cold and lonely; and here was the ship, so firm and well lighted and warm." On the promenade deck, steward Arthur Lewis saw three ladies strolling arm and arm and pleaded with them to get into a lifeboat. "'We're alright Steward, the ship can't sink,'" they told him, and "'we don't want to go down in one of those little boats.'" Passengers believed, said Mr. D. H. Bishop, "that there was no danger, and the general feeling was that those who had put off were making fools of themselves and would have the trouble of rowing back to the boat again after a few hours." Stewards, too, oblivious to the graveness of the situation, were readying the dining saloon tables for breakfast. The ship's band, dressed in a mix of blue coats and white jackets, were playing "Great Big Beautiful Doll," "Alexander's Ragtime Band," and other merry, fast-paced tunes. There was a "sense of the whole thing being a dream . . . that those who walked the decks or tied one another's lifebelts on were actors in a scene . . . that the dream would end soon and we should wake up. . . ."

Eventually, however, many women were picked up bodily by crewmen and dropped into the lifeboats. Their husbands hurriedly kissed them good-bye, expecting to follow them in another lifeboat or to rejoin them in New York.

While on the port side only women and children were generally permitted in the lifeboats, on the starboard side, men were allowed to climb in if there were no women in sight. On both sides of the ship, however, very few of the lifeboats were loaded anywhere near to their capacity. Officers at first refused to fill them, fearing the boats would buckle under the weight as they dropped down to the sea. Henry Harper remembered stepping into a lifeboat holding his pet Pekinese spaniel, Sun Yat Sen. "There seemed to be lots of room," he remarked, "and nobody made any objection."

At 12:45 A.M., lifeboat 7, with a capacity of sixty-five, was lowered into the water with just twenty-eight people aboard. At the same time, Quartermaster George Rowe began firing distress rockets every five or six minutes, and with that, many passengers at last began sensing the danger they were in. In the third-class dining saloon, a crowd of passengers, many clutching rosaries, had gathered solemnly in prayer. And as lifeboat 5 descended, loaded to capacity, four men brazenly jumped into it; one, weighing 250 pounds, fell on top of a woman passenger, knocking her unconscious and dislocating two of her ribs.

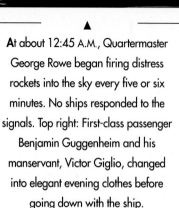

At about 12:45 A.M., Quartermaster George Rowe began firing distress rockets into the sky every five or six minutes. No ships responded to the signals. Top right: First-class passenger Benjamin Guggenheim and his manservant, Victor Giglio, changed into elegant evening clothes before going down with the ship.

Many others, however, resisted the urge to panic. Isidor and Ida Straus came near lifeboat 8 as it was being loaded. Mr. Straus declared he would not get in until all women and children had been safely taken off the boat. Mrs. Straus then refused to leave her husband's side, stating, "We have been living together for many years, and where you go, I go." After giving her fur coat to her maid, who descended in the boat, she and her husband sat down in steamer chairs and calmly watched as the lifeboats filled. Benjamin Guggenheim and his manservant, Victor Giglio, removed their life jackets and changed into elegant evening clothes before returning to the deck. He told a steward, "I think there is grave doubt that the men will get off. I am willing to remain and play the man's game if there are not enough boats for more than the women and children. I won't die here like a beast. Tell my wife . . . I played the game out straight and to the end. No woman shall be left aboard this ship because Ben Guggenheim is a coward." Major Butt and Frank Millet chose to retire to the first-class smoking room, where they sat at a table and played a final hand of cards before going their own way.

This discharge book of *Titanic* steward Percy Keene noted that he had unceremoniously been relieved of duty without pay on April 15, 1912. The reason given was "Vessel lost." Keene survived and returned to the sea the following month on the *Oceanic*.

At 2:17 A.M., the *Titanic*'s stern rose out of the water (above and following spread), reaching a near vertical position before the great ship disappeared under the sea. From the lifeboats, passengers heard a hideous noise as all the contents of the ship crashed forward. Several survivors reported seeing the ship begin to break apart.

Lifeboats were still leaving the ship only partly filled. At 1:10 A.M., lifeboat 1, with a capacity of forty, was lowered with only twelve passengers aboard. Lifeboat 13, however, was loaded nearly to capacity. Lawrence Beesley had been permitted to climb in after all the women and children in sight had boarded. The descent, he remembered, was a great adventure: "It was exciting to feel the boat sink by jerks, foot by foot, . . . thrilling to see the black hull of the ship on one side and the sea, seventy feet below, on the other, or to pass down by cabins and saloons, brilliantly lighted." To leading stoker Fred Barrett, a fellow passenger, the eerily still *Titanic* looked like "a great lighted theater." Twelve-year-old Ruth Becker was also aboard lifeboat 13. As the boat pulled away from the side of the *Titanic*, she remembered, "we could see the water rushing into the ship. Rowing away, looking at the *Titanic*, it was a beautiful sight outlined against the starry sky, every porthole and saloon blazing with light. It was impossible to think anything could be wrong with such an enormous ship, were it not for the tilt downwards toward the bow."

Fear was increasing on the *Titanic* as her forward section listed ever deeper in the water. Five minutes after lifeboat

▲

Two little brothers, three-year-old Michel (left) and two-year-old Edmond, had come aboard the *Titanic* with their father, who had listed himself as "M. Hoffman." As the *Titanic* sank, their father wrapped the toddlers in a blanket and handed them to a woman in a lifeboat. In New York, the boys were cared for by a survivor, Miss Margaret Hays, before being reunited with their mother, Mme. Marcelle Navratil (above). Their father, Michel Navratil, it turned out, had kidnapped the boys during divorce proceedings and spirited them onto the *Titanic* under the name of "Hoffman." Michel, interviewed in 1996 at the age of eighty-seven, recalled the unpleasant experience of being placed inside a sack and raised aboard the rescue ship *Carpathia*.

13 descended, panicked passengers attempted to rush crowded lifeboat 14, which already had sixty aboard. The attempt was halted when Fifth Officer Lowe fired his revolver three times down the ship's side as a warning. A young boy, however, had managed to leap into the boat and crawled under a seat to hide. Charlotte Collyer and other women covered him with their skirts, but Officer Lowe dragged him to his feet and ordered him out, threatening him with his revolver. The boy climbed out of the lifeboat while the women sobbed.

Although the captain had ordered some of the lifeboats to "stand by" in the water, most rowed away quickly from the ship for fear that "suction" would drag them under as the ship sank. Afloat in their tiny boats on the immense sea, lifeboat passengers watched as the *Titanic*'s lights blazed at an unreal angle and her bow plunged beneath the surface at 1:15. On board the sinking ship, as water crept up foot by foot, the gymnasium instructor was, incredibly, still helping passengers on the mechanical exercise equipment. The orchestra continued to calm the crowd with waltzes, ragtime, and music hall tunes, and last drinks were "on the house" in the first-class smoking room.

The reality of the disaster, however, was keener in the boiler and engine rooms below, where workers bravely stayed at their posts to provide enough power to keep the *Titanic*'s lights burning and the great ship's wireless operating. In boiler room 5, a few firemen were helping two of their fellow crewmen, Herbert Harvey and Jonathan Shepherd, handle the pumps when Shepherd stumbled into an open manhole and broke his leg. The injured engineer was made as comfortable as possible while the others returned to their tasks. Suddenly, sea water rushed in as the bulkhead between boiler rooms 5 and 6 collapsed. Most made it up the safety ladder, but Shepherd and Harvey perished in the flood.

Up on deck, the last wooden life-boat, number 4, was being readied shortly before two o'clock, and John Jacob Astor handed his pregnant wife into the boat. After the millionaire was refused permission to join her, he helped other women climb aboard, then stood on deck and waved as it descended only 15 feet down to the water, instead of the usual 70-foot distance. Only the collapsible lifeboats now remained. After assisting passengers, J. Bruce Ismay made his escape in collapsible boat C, the last boat launched from the starboard side. More than fifteen hundred terrified men, women, and children remained aboard the doomed *Titanic*. Realizing their desperation, Lightoller ordered the crew to form a circle around collapsible D, the last lifeboat, and to permit only women and children to board the boat. A Frenchman who had listed himself as "M. Hoffman" passed his two little boys, Michel and Edmond, to the crew, and collapsible D got away at 2:05.

At that moment, the captain told the wireless operators and other crew members that they had done their duty and should look to their own safety. Marconi operator John Phillips, however, stayed at his post, as did thirty-four engineers, plumbers, electricians, and boiler room employees. On deck, a group of men struggled to release collapsible B from its lashings on top of the deckhouse, and a man climbed above the crowd on a chain or coil of rope, his hands stretched out as if in benediction. In steerage, "Hundreds were in a circle with a preacher in the middle, praying, crying." Others fell or jumped from the ship, hoping to swim to one of the lifeboats. At 2:10 the ship's bow lunged deeper into the water, sending the sea washing over the deck. "When the forward part of the ship dropped suddenly at a faster rate," recalled a lifeboat passenger, " . . . there was a sudden rush of passengers on all decks toward the stern. It was like a wave. We could see the great black mass of

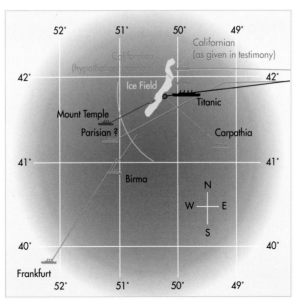

▲
The *Titanic* was not alone that night in the North Atlantic. This illustration, from information by the United States Hydrographic Office and wireless communication in the area, shows the position of the *Titanic* and other ships negotiating the icefields.

people in the steerage sweeping to the rear part of the boat and breaking through in the upper decks." Young Jack Thayer had dived into the water and clung for safety to the overturned collapsible B, which had been washed overboard before it could be launched. From the freezing water, he watched "groups of the almost fifteen hundred people still aboard, clinging in clusters or bunches, like swarming bees; only to fall in masses, pairs or singly, as the great after part of the ship, two hundred and fifty feet of it, rose into the sky. . . ."

On deck, J. Collins, a cook, saw a weeping woman rushing toward him, carrying a child. "I took the child from the woman and made for one of the boats," Collins recalled. Seconds later, a huge wave washed the child out of his arms, and he and the woman were swept off the ship into the sea. People were hurled back "in a dreadful, huddled mass," Lightoller remembered. "Those that didn't disappear under the water right away, instinctively started to clamber up that part of the deck still out of water, and work their way towards the stern." The ship's orchestra had continued to play as the deck heaved higher in the air. Now, bandleader Wallace Hartley released his fellow musicians, but none of

Wallace Hartley, the *Titanic's* bandleader continued to conduct his musicians as the ship began to sink. Even after he had released them near the end, all remained together and continued to play. Hartley and every one of the musicians perished. Top: A drawing by Henry Hutt dedicated to the memory of the *Titanic's* orchestra.

them made a move to leave. Instead, they played a final, solemn tune as the water rolled up the deck. Some said it was "Autumn," others remembered the hymn "Nearer My God to Thee."

At 2:17 A.M., the *Titanic's* stern abruptly rose out of the water, pivoted, and stopped in a vertical position. The leviathan's brilliant lights at last went out, then flickered again with a ghostly crimson glow before going dark again three minutes later. From the lifeboats, passengers heard a hideous, stupefying noise as the contents of the ship crashed forward—"partly a roar, partly a groan, partly a rattle, and partly a smash," like "all the heavy things one could think of" hurtling from one end of the ship to the other—a long, unearthly death groan that could be heard for miles. The *Titanic's* gigantic propellers hung over the water, and her forward funnel toppled under the strain, crushing dozens who were struggling in the sea. Finally, the ship eased down into the water with a gurgling sound, "like a stricken animal," trailing steam and soot and leaving behind, finally, only a smoky mist over a sea as quiet as a lake of oil.

As the great *Titanic* sank, Colonel Gracie found himself trapped inside a whirlpool and dragged far down in the knifelike 28-degree water. After breaking away and swimming to the surface,

At 7:00 A.M. on April 15, lifeboats approached the Cunard liner *Carpathia*, which had heard the *Titanic*'s distress call at midnight and sped through the night to her position. By 8:00 A.M., the *Carpathia* had taken all of the *Titanic*'s 705 survivors aboard; 1,523 passengers and crew members lost their lives in the disaster.

▲

Crowds waited for news of the disaster outside
the White Star Line offices in New York.

▲

A throng gathered near Cunard's New York pier
(left, rear) hoping to catch a glimpse of the
Titanic's survivors arriving aboard the *Carpathia*.

▲

On April 18, 1912, the *Carpathia* docked at New York's Pier 54, after leaving the *Titanic*'s lifeboats off at White Star Piers 58 and 59. The dazed survivors emerged into the glare of photographers' flash powder and worldwide publicity. Left: This landing card was issued by the *Carpathia* to identify survivor Gilbert M. Tucker, Jr., of Albany, New York, as a *Titanic* passenger.

he remembered, "I could see no *Titanic* in sight. . . . There was only a slight gulp behind me as the water closed over her." Gracie finally spotted the overturned collapsible boat on which Jack Thayer, Lightoller, and more than a dozen other men hung for life in the freezing sea. Gracie and other swimmers pulled themselves aboard, and soon there were thirty souls aboard the partly submerged boat, including a woman, third-class passenger Mrs. Rosa Abbott. She had been thrown into the sea with both her sons; although the boys were lost, she had managed to swim to safety aboard the capsized boat. "One more clambering aboard would have swamped our already crowded craft," Gracie recalled; those on board used oars to strike swimmers who attempted to climb on. Some aboard were frozen, and two dead were thrown over the side. Hundreds of others, swimming alone in the freezing sea, shrieked and moaned as they slowly froze to death. Jack Thayer heard their horrible cries as "one continuous wailing chant . . . like locusts on a midsummer night." The unbearable screams gradually died away, "as one after another could no longer stand the cold and exposure."

For an hour, the partially filled lifeboats stood by, and none rowed back to offer help. Finally, after "the yells and shrieks had subsided," Fifth Officer Lowe moved passengers from his crowded lifeboat 14 into other boats, and he and Scarrett rowed back to see if any in the water could be saved. When they got to the wreckage, "the sight we saw was awful," Scarrett recalled. Hundreds of dead bodies floated in their life belts. After turning many over in the water, they could only see four alive. "The first one we picked up was a male passenger. He died shortly after we got him in the boat. After a hard struggle we managed to get the other three. One of these we saw kneeling in prayer upon what appeared to be part of a staircase. . . . All the bodies we saw seemed as if they had perished with the cold as their limbs were all cramped up. As we left that awful scene we gave way to tears. It was enough to break the stoutest heart."

Only fourteen people who went down on the *Titanic* were pulled out of the water, and only half of those survived. In lifeboat 3, women who had lost their husbands and fathers called out their loved ones' names as they neared the other lifeboats, asking, "Are you there?" The answer, a passenger recalled, was always, "No."

At 4:30, dawn at last began to break, revealing the tiny lifeboats adrift in fields of ice, surrounded by towering bergs, some the height of the *Titanic*. One—spotted by a passing ship later that day—had a scar of red paint along its base. The sea had turned rough, but one by one the ragtag fleet of lifeboats rowed gratefully toward

▲

Survivors taken aboard the *Carpathia* were warmly comforted and cared for by the Cunard ship's passengers and crew. Right: A medal presented to the officers and crew of the *Carpathia* by the survivors of the *Titanic*.

rescue. The Cunard liner *Carpathia* had finally arrived, after hearing the *Titanic*'s plea for help and speeding through the night toward her position. By 8:30, all of the survivors—many of them soaking wet and frightened, their bodies rigid with the cold—had groped their way up rope ladders or were hauled in slings to the *Carpathia*'s deck, while children were put into canvas sacks and pulled aboard. Comforted by warm food, blankets, borrowed clothing, and the caring ministrations of the *Carpathia*'s passengers and crew, the stunned survivors slowly came to grips with the scope of the personal losses they had suffered. Of the *Titanic*'s 2,228 passengers and crew, only 705 were rescued; 1,523 men, women, and children—friends and loved ones—had perished when the *Titanic* had gone down. At last, on Thursday, April 18, after three more anguished days at sea, the witnesses to the disaster ended their nightmarish journey in New York, where the public waited desperately, disbelievingly, for news. While reporters and photographers mobbed the dazed survivors on the pier, a cable ship—the *Mackay-Bennett* from Halifax, Nova Scotia—was already steaming toward the site of the *Titanic*'s sinking to recover victims' bodies from the sea.

BENEFIT PERFORMANCE
FOR THE FAMILIES OF THE VICTIMS
of the
"TITANIC" DISASTER

The Twenty-Ninth of April, 1912
METROPOLITAN OPERA HOUSE
NEW YORK

▲

Two weeks after the disaster, New Yorkers attended a special performance at the Metropolitan Opera to benefit survivors.

Two days later, on Saturday, April 20, the German liner *Bremen* passed within a few miles of where the *Titanic* had gone down. "It was a beautiful afternoon," recalled a woman passenger, "and the sun glistening on the big iceberg was a wonderful picture." As the ship drew nearer, however, those aboard could make out small dots floating in the sea. A "feeling of awe and sadness crept over every one, and the ship proceeded in absolute silence." Looking down over the rail, passengers "distinctly saw a number of bodies so clearly that we could make out what they were wearing, and whether they were men or women. We saw one woman in her nightdress with a baby clasped closely to her breast. . . . There was another woman, fully dressed, with her arms tight around the body of a shaggy dog that looked like a St. Bernard. The bodies of three men, all in a group, all clinging to one steamer chair floated close by, and just beyond them were a dozen bodies of men, all in life-preservers, clinging together as though in the last desperate struggle for life. . . . We could see the white life preservers of many more dotting the sea. . . . The scene," she said, "moved everyone on board to the point of tears. . . . "

▲

The *Titanic*'s surviving wireless operator, Harold Bride, had to be carried down *Carpathia*'s gangway, his severely frostbitten and smashed feet swathed in bandages.

◄

First saloon steward Thomas Whiteley (right) survived the sinking, although he had broken his leg when it became entangled in the ropes of a lifeboat as it was being lowered.

THE "TITANIC" DISASTER

WHEN THE "CARPATHIA" CAME IN

SOME OF THOSE WHO RETURNED

▲

For weeks after the sinking, newspapers and magazines were filled with gripping accounts of the disaster and the personal stories of survivors.

VICTIMS OF THE TITANIC

Among the passengers and crew members mentioned in the previous pages, the survivors were Rosa Stanton Abbott, Madeleine Force Astor, lead fireman Frederick Barrett, steward George Beauchamp, Ruth Becker, Lawrence Beesley, Ellen Bird (Ida Straus's maid), Dickinson H. Bishop, Fourth Officer Joseph Groves Boxhall, wireless operator Harold Bride, Margaret "Molly" Tobin Brown, Edith Brown, Elizabeth Brown, Helen Churchill Hungerford Candee, Charlotte Drake Cardeza, John Collins, Charlotte Collyer, Cosmo Edmund Duff Gordon, Lucile Wallace Sutherland Duff Gordon, Elizabeth Mussey Eustis, Frederick Fleet, Colonel Archibald Gracie, IV, Henry Sleeper Harper, Irene "Rene" Wallach Harris, Esther Hart, Eva Hart, Margaret Bechstein Hayes, Frederick Maxfield Hoyt, Abraham Hyman, Joseph Bruce Ismay, steward James Johnson, Carl Jonsson, steward Percy Keene, Reginald R. Lee, steward Arthur Lewis, Second Officer Charles H. Lightoller, Fifth Officer Harold G. Lowe, Edmond Roger Navratil (aka Edmond Hoffman), Michel Marcel Navratil (aka Michel Hoffman), fireman John Podesta, Quartermaster George Rowe, Emily Maria Borie Ryerson, Able Seaman Joseph Scarrett, Elizabeth W. Shutes, Mary Eloise Hughes Smith, Frederic Oakley Spedden, Margaretta Corning Stone Spedden, Robert Douglas Spedden, Martha Eustis Stephenson, John "Jack" Borland Thayer Jr., Gilbert Milligan Tucker Jr., Ella Holmes White, steward Thomas Whiteley, Eleanor Elkins Widener, Hugh Woolner.

Those who did not survive were Eugene Joseph Abbott, Rossmore Edward Abbott, Thomas Andrews, Colonel John Jacob Astor, band member Theodore Ronald Brailey, band member Roger Marie Bricoux, Thomas William Solomon Brown, Major Archibald Willingham Butt, Reverend Ernest Courtenay Carter, band member John Frederick Preston Clarke, Patrick Dooley, Victor Giglio, Benjamin Guggenheim, postal clerk William Logan Gwinn, Benjamin Hart, band master Wallace Henry Hartley, Herbert G. Harvey, Charles Melville Hays, engineer John Henry Hesketh, band member John Law Hume, band member George Alexander Krins, postal clerk John Starr March, T. W. McCrawley, Francis Davis Millet, Sixth Officer James Paul Moody, First Officer William M. Murdoch, Michel Navratil (aka M. Hoffman), steward James Arthur Paintin, wireless operator John G. Phillips, Franz Pulbaum, Jonathan Shepherd, Captain Edward John Smith, James Clinch Smith, postal clerk John Richard Jargo Smith, fireman "Gus" A. Stanbrook, William Thomas Stead, Ida Blun Straus, Isidor Straus, Henry Sutehall, Jr., band member Percy Cornelius Taylor, John Borland Thayer, Harry Elkins Widener, George Duton Widener, Chief Officer Henry Tingle Wilde, postal clerk James Bertram Williamson, band member John Westley Woodward, postal clerk Oscar S. Woody.

A complete list of the Titanic *disaster victims and survivors is included at the beginning and ending of this book.*

IN SEARCH OF THE TITANIC

THE GRIM WATERS OF the North Atlantic had barely closed over the *Titanic*—and the *Mackay-Bennett*, loaded with coffins, was still searching for victims adrift on the cold seas—when the first plans were laid to find the wreck of the lost liner. Only five days after the agonizing tragedy, John Jacob Astor's son Vincent announced his intention to locate and blow up the *Titanic*'s hull to retrieve the missing body of his father. His plan was abandoned the next day, when the men of the *Mackay-Bennett* finally recovered the millionaire's battered remains. Others, however, still dreamed of finding the *Titanic*'s wreck. Lost in total darkness 12,460 feet below the waves, the *Titanic* continued to fire and torment the public's imagina-

▲

The *Titanic*'s foremast lamp, one of two which indicated the ship's direction, was recovered in 1987. Left: The wreck's majestic bow was captured on 70mm IMAX® film in the summer of 1991 by an international team lead by film producer and director Stephen Low and the P. P. Shirshov Institute of Oceanography in Moscow, Russia.

tion. The location of her sinking—an imprecisely known patch of the Atlantic, vacant and menacing, some 450 miles southeast of Newfoundland—became part of the world's moral geography. Unknown and unreachable, her abyssal grave and her fatal voyage obsessed dreamers and adventurers for more than seven decades.

Since the *Titanic* plunged to the deep bottom of the sea, there have been successive plans, some imaginative and farfetched, to find and even retrieve the fabled wreck. Many of the schemes were fueled by persistent rumors that the *Titanic* carried a precious load of gems and gold. The legends continued, despite the fact that her cargo manifest and insurance claims filed after the sinking made clear that there was nothing in the least extravagant about her freight. All thoughts of finding her, from the beginning, have been complicated by the treacherous weather of the North Atlantic and the vast depth to which the *Titanic* sank. She rests two and a half miles below the surface, where the water pressure is 6,000 pounds per square inch—enough to implode almost any diving vessel and crush its passengers to dust. Confounding further any hope of locating the great ship were the conflicting records of her last estimated position—based on inexact celestial calculations confused by possible misjudgments of her speed, the time, the currents, and the winds.

Nevertheless, the very year she sank, the Astor, Widener, and Guggenheim families jointly investigated the possibility of finding and raising the *Titanic*'s hull—even going so far as to contract with the Merritt and Chapman Derrick and Wrecking Company for the work. The firm, however, correctly determined that they lacked the technology in 1912 to recover a ship at so deep and dangerous a site. The next year, however, an intrepid Denver architect named Charles Smith came up with an innovative plan to find the wreck. His scheme called for fitting a submarine with electromagnets that would be attracted to the *Titanic*'s metal hull. Smith reckoned that he would then raise the enormous ship by fixing other magnets onto the wreck itself. To

▲

In 1903, an Italian engineer designed this submersible device. Although it could not function at great depths, it had many features in common with the advanced submersibles used today.

these he intended to attach cables, and a barge would then winch the *Titanic* to the surface. The plan, Smith calculated, would require exactly 162 men and a budget of $1.5 million. It was quickly dropped—as was a similar plan put forward by another magnet enthusiast. This second proposal would use magnets to attach empty pontoons to the imense wreck. The floats would then rise balloonlike to the surface, towing the *Titanic* with them.

After these preliminary schemes, curiosity about the *Titanic* was overshadowed by the colossal traumas of the Great Depression and two world wars. The lure of the doomed ship almost faded from memory until 1953. In the summer of that year, a British marine salvage firm, Risdon Beasley Ltd., began a quiet hunt for the *Titanic*'s wreck. The salvors took a vessel out to the site at 43°65' N, 52°04' W and deployed high explosives to generate an echo image of the ocean bottom, but they failed to locate the ship. Two years later, Walter Lord published his acclaimed book about the *Titanic*'s sinking, *A Night to Remember*—followed by the release of the British film in 1958—and *Titanic* fever was rekindled. Nevertheless, search attempts were few over the next decade, and attention mainly focused on a $5-million scheme concocted in 1966 by a young English hosiery worker named Douglas Woolley. With no scientific training but a knack for publicity, Woolley proposed to surround the hull of the *Titanic* with hundreds of water-filled plastic containers. He then planned to run electricity through them in order to release gases that would lift the huge ship to the surface. Another of Woolley's proposals called for raising the hulk by rigging it with air-filled nylon balloons. Despite the considerable media attention, Woolley was unable to raise the funds to pursue his dreams. No more serious plans to locate or recover the *Titanic* were announced until the 1970s, when the persistent Woolley founded the Titanic Salvage Company, asserted he had claim to the wreck, and generated great publicity by proclaiming his intention to find, raise, and tow the *Titanic* into Liverpool, where he would restore her as a floating museum. Despite several attempts during the decade to assemble the technical expertise and financing to pull off his scheme, Woolley never once traveled to the wreck site, and he was never able to raise the £2 million that would have been necessary to begin his salvage attempt.

Other dreamers besides Woolley were at the same time concocting plans to find and recover the *Titanic*. Most assumed that the ship was intact on the seabed with all her splendor preserved, thanks to the lack of oxygen and the intense cold at the deep bottom of the ocean. One strategist, an English haulage contractor named Arthur Hickey, proposed freezing the inside of the ship's hull so that she would float to the surface of

▲

Scripps Institution oceanographer Dr. Fred Spiess (left) planned the technical aspects of a 1980 expedition to locate the *Titanic* led by film producer Mike Harris (right). The expedition was not successful.

the ocean, much like a giant ice cube. The freezing theory was also favored by a would-be salvager named John Pierce. He hoped to drape a nitrogen-filled net around the *Titanic* which would freeze her and float her up to the surface. A third adventurer proposed filling the *Titanic*'s hull with Ping-Pong balls, which he believed would lift her gently from the ocean bed. A fourth dreamed of raising the *Titanic* by injecting her hull with 180,000 tons of molten wax, which, after hardening, would supposedly float the wreck up to the surface. Walt Disney Productions even studied the feasibility of using a 51-foot deep-water submersible vessel to dive to the wreck and film her. And the British industrialist Sir James Goldsmith also backed a plan to find and photograph the sunken liner. Like Woolley, however, none of these organizers were able to secure enough financing to put their theories to the test.

By the end of the 1970s, however, new advances in computer science, sonar, and electronic deep-sea search technology had made the discovery of the *Titanic* technically feasible for the first time. The first serious, scientifically based search for the legendary ship was launched in 1980 by a Texas oil magnate named Jack Grimm. A "searcher for lost legends," Grimm had previously financed expeditions to find the Loch Ness monster, Noah's Ark, and Bigfoot. His attention now turned to the *Titanic*, and to find the fabled wreck he joined up with film producer and expedition leader Mike Harris and a scientific team from Columbia University's Lamont-Doherty Geological Observatory. The well-thought-out expedition included two of the world's best oceanographers, Lamont-Doherty geologist Dr. William Ryan and Scripps Institution oceanographer Dr. Fred Spiess. Ryan had calculated that the *Titanic* likely lay within a 600-square-mile zone of the North Atlantic, based on her last reported position and her potential speed and drift. Grimm's thirty-eight-member scientific team chartered the vessel *H.J.W. Fay*, loaded it with advanced equipment, including underwater cameras and side-scan sonar to detect large objects on the seabed, and set out from Florida to the target area. Using sonar images, the team scrutinized the ocean bottom and identified fourteen possible sites where the wreck might lie. Unfortunately, however, bad weather and equipment difficulties thwarted their search. Despite the failure of this first attempt, Grimm remained determined to locate the *Titanic*. In 1981, he and Harris set out on a second search, this time aboard the U.S. Navy's research vessel *Gyre*. The 297-ton ship was equipped with magnetometers, sophisticated deep-tow side-scan sonar developed by Scripps, and advanced navigational gear from NASA. If Grimm succeeded in finding the *Titanic*, he

▲

At a 1981 press conference in Boston, following his second unsuccessful expedition to find the *Titanic*, Jack Grimm (at microphone) displays photographs and a diagram of the search area in the North Atlantic. Right: The red dot on this ocean map indicates the approximate location of the *Titanic*. The wreckage sits on the seabed at a depth of 12,600 feet in underwater terrain near the Grand Banks of Newfoundland.

planned to use *Aluminaut*, a deep-water submersible created by Reynolds Aluminum, to dive down to it, explore it, and recover artifacts, believing the persistent legends that the sunken hull hid a cache of gold and treasure.

Aboard the *Gyre*, scientists refined their estimates of the *Titanic*'s likely location, based on her last telegraphed position, her speed and direction after encountering the iceberg, reports from other ships, and a host of other factors. Based on their analysis, they determined that the *Titanic* most likely lay where the continent rises from the ocean floor southeast of Newfoundland, in an area they dubbed Titanic Canyon. Although the region had previously been surveyed by the U.S. Navy, and despite repeated sonar searches of the target sites, the *Gyre* team failed to discover the *Titanic*'s wreck, bedeviled by high seas and heavy rainstorms. In July 1983, the undaunted Grimm set off on a third expedition, this time aboard the U.S. Navy vessel *Robert D. Conrad*. This final attempt, too, was hampered by fierce winds, 30-foot seas, and malfunctioning gear. It yielded nothing. Grimm had financed three failed expeditions at a cost of $2 million.

Now that Grimm's high-profile searches had proved expensive failures, opportunity was ripe for others to pick up the *Titanic*'s trail. By 1985, prospects had improved because deep-water

exploration and photography technology had reached new levels of sophistication. Scientists at the French Navy's oceanographic agency, Institut Francais de Recherche pour l'Exploitation des Mers (IFREMER), had developed particularly effective side-scan sonar capabilities, and the U.S. Navy had spent nearly $3 million constructing a 4,000-pound, unmanned, deep-towed submersible device called *Argo*, equipped with advanced video camera and strobe lighting equipment. To jointly test the new equipment, French and American scientists collaborated in a two-month-long North Atlantic expedition in the summer of 1985. The first objective of the mission was to test the new technology; the second was to find and photograph the *Titanic*.

Plans called for the French vessel, *Le Suroit*, to tow the new torpedo-shaped, deep-search side-scan sonar device, called SAR, 600 feet above the ocean floor. With SAR, the French team—headed by IFREMER oceanographer Jean-Louis Michel and operations leader Jean Jarry—would explore an area 400 nautical square miles in size, where Michel had determined, through painstaking research, that the *Titanic* probably lay. In a process called "mowing the lawn," SAR would scan the search area in passes three-fifths of a mile wide, producing

high-resolution images that resembled black-and-white photographs of the ocean bottom. The team would also employ a magnetometer to distinguish between rocks and metal objects they observed on the sea floor. The expedition plan called for the French sonar system to locate the *Titanic*. After that, the joint team would use the Americans' video-based search system, under a U.S. Navy grant, to explore and photograph the wreck.

But after repetitively passing over 80 percent of the search area for twenty-one days, twenty-four hours a day, in mercilessly heavy seas, the sonar technology turned up no evidence of the *Titanic*. The disappointed French and American teams transferred to the U.S. Navy vessel *Knorr* and, while *Le Suroit* headed back to France, resumed the hunt using the Americans' advanced video search system: three ultrasensitive video cameras mounted on *Argo*, capable of seeing in extremely low light conditions. For this part of the mission, the team decided to focus on a still-unexamined portion of Jean-Louis Michel's search area. The French oceanographer knew from experience that sinking ships scatter debris along the ocean floor as they drop, so Robert D. Ballard—geologist and leader of the American expedition team—decided to

By the late 1970s and early '80s, improvements in deep-ocean technology made the discovery of the *Titanic*'s wreck technically feasible for the first time. The illustration above shows the interior of *Argo*, an unmanned submersible device equipped with video cameras that recorded in 1985 the first images of the sunken *Titanic*. Left: In this 1981 schematic, the pink arc and triangles show the range of the yellow *Argo*'s sonar capabilities; the green trapezoids indicate the areas that *Argo* could visually search with its five cameras.

employ the visual system to hunt for the *Titanic*'s debris field as well as for the wreck itself.

The team's sweeps of the target area went on monotonously for fourteen days, turning up nothing but endless images of sandy seabed, dunes, and rat-tailed fish. But at five minutes past one o'clock on the morning of September 1, 1985, the video monitor in the control room began displaying images of a huge, man-made object on the ocean bottom. It was one of the *Titanic*'s giant boilers, expelled from a boiler room as the liner sank and now, seventy-three years later, captured by the strobe lights and sensitive video cameras aboard *Argo*. Soon, tangled pieces of steel plating, railings, and portholes became visible on the *Knorr*'s video screen, and Michel, watching the dramatic images appear, realized that they had at last found the *Titanic*. A crew member was sent to inform Ballard of the discovery. By then it was nearly two o'clock in the morning, close to the time when the great ship had taken her final plunge on the cold morning of April 15, 1912. Spontaneously, the crew assembled on the stern of the *Knorr* for a moment of silence in the calm, clear, star-filled night and raised the company flag of Harland and Wolff as a tribute to the *Titanic* and her lost passengers and crew.

The next day, the team sent *Argo* down for a second, more extensive exploration of the site. Her cameras revealed the *Titanic* resting upright, apparently intact on the sea bottom, and her bow seemed still stunningly preserved and lodged deep in

FIRST VIEW OF THE TITANIC

The very first view of the *Titanic* upon its discovery (right) showed one of her giant boilers, located in the early morning of September 1, 1985. Below right are the *Titanic*'s boilers as they appeared in the builder's shop. Below: These diagrams depict the areas searched by SAR and *Argo* before the discovery of the *Titanic*. Following page: The U.S. Navy vessel *Knorr* and its successful expedition crew in 1985.

Argo coverage of Titanic canyon and vicinity
ARGO SEARCH—PHASE I

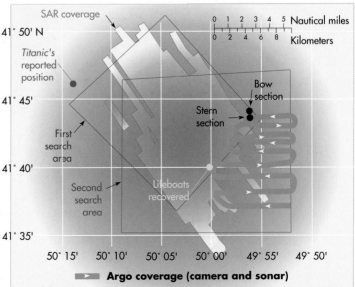
ARGO SEARCH—PHASE II
Argo coverage (camera and sonar)

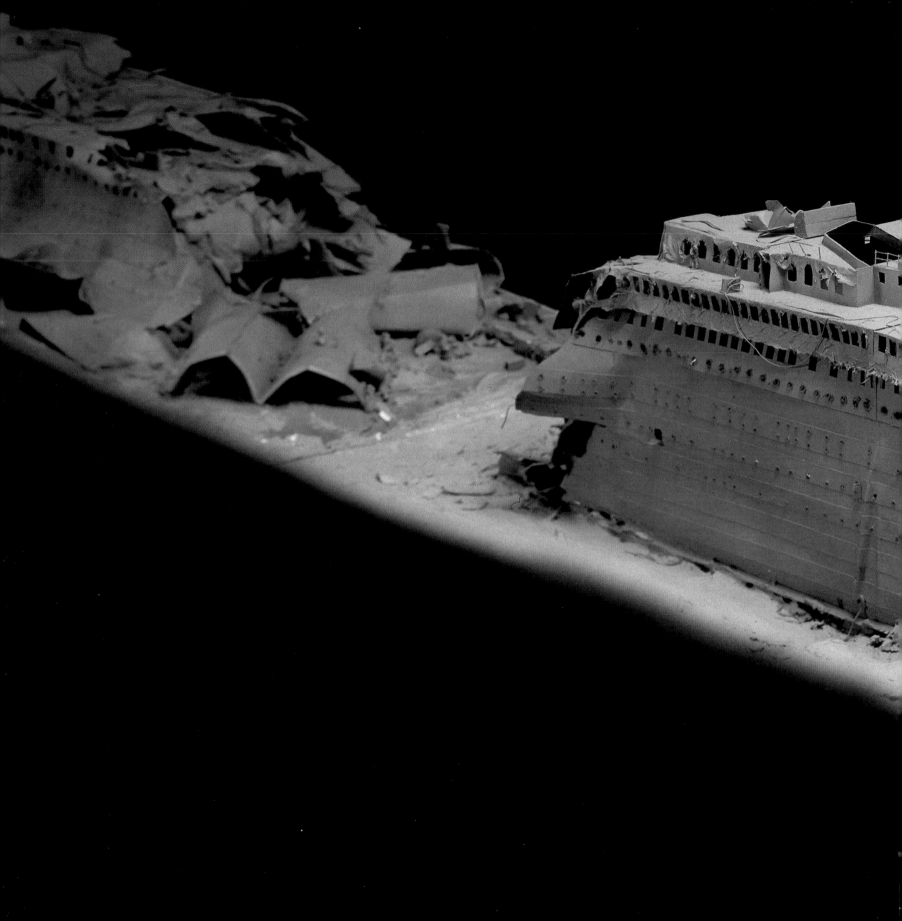

This model of the *Titanic* shows the ship resting on the seabed (not in her actual position). The two main parts of her hull are separated in reality by 2,000 feet.

Argo is launched from the *Knorr* on one
of her numerous dives to explore and
photograph the wreck site.

ocean-bottom silt. To get even more detailed, close-up images, the team decided to lower a 2-ton towed device called ANGUS (Acoustically Navigated Geophysical Underwater Survey) and position it in close proximity to the *Titanic*'s wreck. Fitted out with 35 mm color cameras, ANGUS took twelve thousand pictures in three dives to the site. Reviewing the film on the way home, the crew discovered that the *Titanic* was not in one piece after all, contrary to what they had earlier reported to the world press, and that her four gigantic funnels had vanished. Her stern had actually come to rest 2,000 feet behind the bow. Around the two sections of the liner lay a vast debris field, almost a square mile in area and strewn with amazingly diverse detritus from the ship, including wine bottles, countless lumps of coal, chamber pots, bedsprings, and cut-glass windows and tiles from the *Titanic*'s luxurious public rooms. Although the wreck was discovered at the very end of the two-month expedition, it turned out that *Le Suroit* had actually passed over the *Titanic* at the very beginning of the search, when the French vessel's magnetometers detected a large metal mass on the seabed. Mistakenly, the scientific team had attributed the surprising readings to equipment problems.

More dismaying to the French researchers,

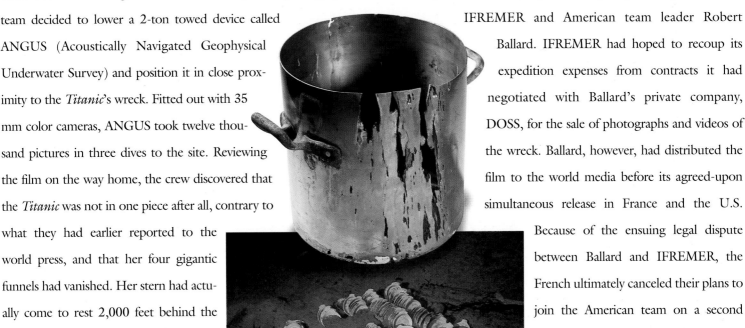

Au gratin dishes stacked just as they had been arranged inside a wooden crate in 1912. The crate has long since disintegrated. Top: The acidity of the ocean-bottom sediment contributed to the corrosion of this cooking pot. Following spread: When the forward section of the ship plowed into the seabed at the high speed of 30 miles an hour or more, the bow was buried in nearly 50 feet of mud.

however, was a contract dispute that quickly developed between IFREMER and American team leader Robert Ballard. IFREMER had hoped to recoup its expedition expenses from contracts it had negotiated with Ballard's private company, DOSS, for the sale of photographs and videos of the wreck. Ballard, however, had distributed the film to the world media before its agreed-upon simultaneous release in France and the U.S. Because of the ensuing legal dispute between Ballard and IFREMER, the French ultimately canceled their plans to join the American team on a second mission to the *Titanic* that had been planned for 1986. This follow-up expedition was to have focused on the testing of French and American deep-sea robotic technology as well as the recovery of artifacts from the *Titanic*'s debris field. In 1985, shortly after the discovery of the wreck, Ballard told a congressional committee that "there is a tremendous amount of material in [the *Titanic*'s] debris area," and that "I am in favor of the recovery of that material probably with manned submarines, to ensure that they are protected and the public and the world have the ability to touch . . . so to speak, and feel the ship." Because American law precludes U.S. naval vessels from participating

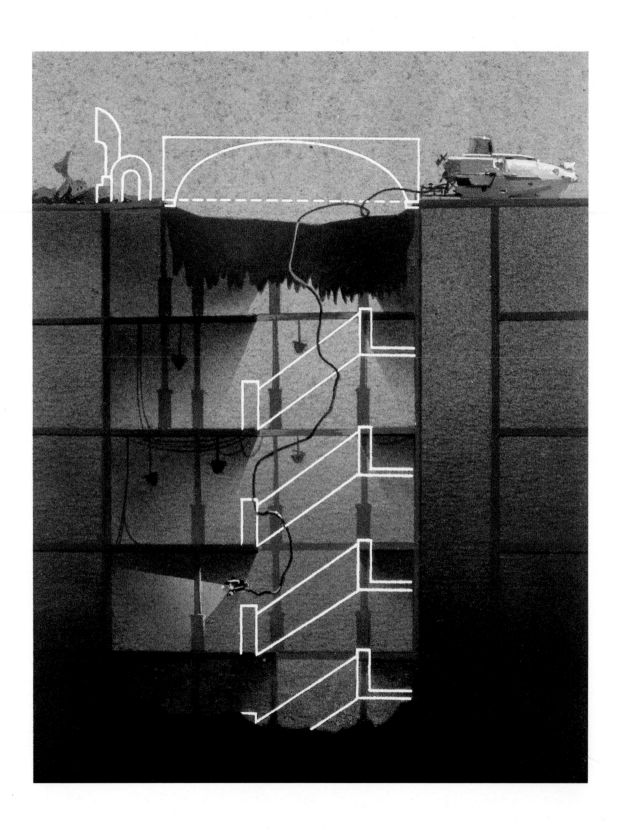

▲

In July 1986, U.S. researchers returned to the *Titanic* with a powerful deep-sea imaging tool—*Jason Jr.*, a 28-inch-long tethered robot packed with high-resolution cameras and powerful lighting. Above: *Jason Jr.* was able to enter the *Titanic's* broken skylight and grand staircase. Once inside the stairway's shell, the robot descended the first few decks, where crystal chandeliers still hung amazingly intact.

in commercial salvage operations, however, the French would have used their advanced, deep-diving submersible vehicle *Nautile* to recover artifacts from the *Titanic* wreck site on the planned second joint expedition, while the U.S. Navy submersible *Alvin* would be used to explore and film the wreck.

In July 1986, however, Ballard's crew of fifty-six returned to the *Titanic* aboard the navy vessel *Atlantis II*—without the French researchers and their artifact-recovery technology but with a more powerful imaging tool than they had had at their disposal the year before: *Jason Jr.* (*J.J.*), a 28-inch-long, tethered, robotic deep-sea exploration vessel. Rigged with high-resolution cameras and powerful lighting, *J.J.* was capable of exploring previously inaccessible regions of the wreck. On July 13, Ballard and two pilots climbed into the three-man, titanium-hulled submersible called *Alvin*, which carried *Jason Jr.* A jellyfish and white-tipped sharks swam by *Alvin*'s window as they descended in a free fall for two and a half hours to the hull of the *Titanic*, two and a half miles below the surface. There, at last, on the bottom loomed the *Titanic*, "a tremendous black wall of steel [that] seemed endless in all directions." Starfish, galathean crabs, and rat-tailed fish now occupied the stately quarters that had once housed millionaires, and great trails of rust, dubbed "rusticles" by Ballard, covered the bow of the ship. Over the next twelve days, *Alvin* made eleven dives to the great wreck, using the tethered robot *J.J.* to enter the broken skylight of the *Titanic*'s grand staircase and descend the first few decks of its empty shell, where large, ghostly crystal chandeliers still hung astonishingly intact. They explored the bow, the hull, the lookout mast, the well deck, and the ship's bridge, drifting over the anchor chains and capstans and the huge holes left by the funnels and glass dome. *J.J.* peered into the gymnasium and the empty officers' quarters and glided over parts of the vast debris field, which resembled a ghostly museum. Scattered across the sands were thousands of everyday objects used by the *Titanic*'s passengers and crew: the ceramic head of a child's doll, a silver bowl, a spittoon, a crystal-and-brass ceiling light fixture, a copper kettle, hundreds of perfectly intact china cups emblazoned with the logo of the White Star Line, a bathtub, a bronze-cast bench end, and thousands of leather shoes. On July 22, the team explored the part of the starboard bow where the iceberg was said to have torn a gash, but they could find no damage above the mud line. Where, they wondered, was the huge tear that the iceberg had inflicted? The silt apparently concealed the evidence, leaving the *Titanic*'s mortal wounds a lingering mystery.

In 1986, the United States Congress passed the Titanic Maritime Memorial Act, calling for a consortium of nations to establish international guidelines and programs "for conducting research on, exploration of, and, if appropriate, salvage of the RMS *Titanic*." Although in his 1985 congressional testimony, Ballard had clearly supported artifact recovery, stating that "I think it would behoove us to move expeditiously to preserve those things that can be recovered," he later radically changed his position, asserting that the *Titanic* site should be left forever undisturbed as a memorial.

That sentiment may have been "a noble thought," reflected the *Titanic* expert and author Walter Lord—but forever, he noted, is a long time. "Pompeii was once the scene of an enormous human tragedy, but now it is a fascinating dig . . . the lure of the ship remains, if only because 'it is there.'" The *Titanic* and her secrets still waited.

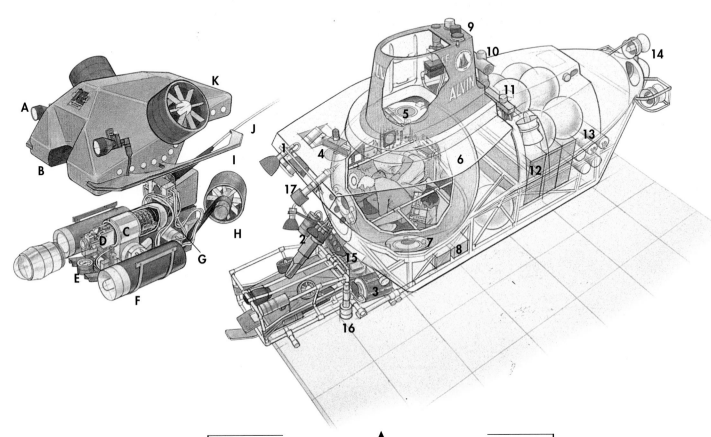

This diagram depicts the advanced search technology of *Alvin* (right) and *Jason Jr.* (left) 1. Still camera. 2. Manipulator arm. 3. Cable winch and reel. 4. Scanning sonar. 5. Hatch. 6. Titanium sphere. 7. Three viewing ports. 8. Jettisonable iron ballast. 9. Acoustic telephone. 10. Hoisting bit. 11. Tanks for air and variable sea water ballast. 12. Batteries. 13. Pressure housing for electric controls. 14. Thrusters. 15. Emergency tether cutter. 16. Down-looking, low-light-level, black-and-white TV camera, or Silicon Intensified Target (SIT) camera. 17. Forward-looking SIT camera. A. Light. B. Foam floatation housing. C. Video camera. D. 35-mm still camera. E. Compass. F. Strobe light. G. Depth Sensor. H. Thruster. I. Docking rail. J. Tether to *Alvin*. K. Reflective disks.

The top of one of the *Titanic*'s boilers was photographed in 1987 on an expedition by Titanic Ventures, now known as RMS Titanic, Inc.
Above: The port side of the *Titanic*'s bow was also photographed in 1987.
Right: A teapot recovered from the debris field in the same year.

ANATOMY OF THE DISASTER

THE *TITANIC* LIES IN DARKNESS on the ocean floor, but her memory has never rested. For nearly a century, endless debates, rumors, speculations, and what ifs have churned up, over and over, every detail of the events of April 1912. Many questions have remained disturbingly unanswered. What damage really occurred when the *Titanic* hit the iceberg? Why did the "unsinkable" leviathan plunge to her doom so quickly? Could the tragedy have been averted? As early as 1919, the writer Joseph Conrad expressed exasperation at the public's unending—even unseemly—curiosity. "What are they after?" he demanded. "What is there for them to find out? We know what has happened. The ship has scraped her side against a piece of ice and sank after floating for two hours and a half, taking a lot of people down with her."

Conrad was correct that the basic facts of the disaster had been well established by exhaustive American and British inquiries held in 1912. The *Titanic* had collided with an iceberg, damage from the glancing blow had caused flooding in at least five watertight compartments, and the great ship could not float with more than four of her six forward compartments filled. Beyond that, however, very little has been understood about the forces and the physical sequence of events that led to the disastrous deaths of 1,523 men, women, and children and the sinking, just five days into her maiden voyage, of the world's most invincible ocean liner. Far from quieting debate, the discovery of the *Titanic*'s wreck in 1985 only led to more unanswered questions. How did the great ship split in two? Why is the bow in near-pristine condition while the stern is a barely recognizable heap of twisted steel? And how long will the rust-encrusted wreck survive in the hostile environment of the ocean floor?

Since Robert Ballard published the location of the wreck in 1987, seven expeditions have traveled to the site with plans to photograph, explore, and investigate the legendary ship and recover artifacts that settled around her on the seabed as she sank. Four of the expeditions—in the summers of 1987, 1993, 1994, and 1996—were organized by RMS Titanic, Inc., a New York–based public company that, in 1992, was awarded sole guardianship rights to the *Titanic* and all materials raised from the wreck by a U.S. federal court judge. On all four of the research and recovery expeditions, RMS Titanic has partnered with IFREMER, the French oceanographic institute that codiscovered the wreck of the *Titanic* in 1985. On these successful operations, the joint team has explored and extensively photographed the wreck site and carefully recovered nearly five thousand artifacts from the vast debris field, many of

which have already been scientifically conserved and exhibited in museums on two continents.

RMS Titanic's 1996 expedition, however, also had a unique scientific purpose. On the expedition, cosponsored by the Discovery Channel, an international group of scientists and engineers from five countries examined the *Titanic*. Using the most sophisticated research tools available and advanced techniques of reverse engineering, forensic science, and crash investigation, they attempted to solve many of the mysteries surrounding the disaster. "The *Titanic* is the subject of a great many myths and a great many bits of misinformation," explained *Titanic* historian Charles Haas. "On this expedition," he added, "we had the opportunity to use the latest scientific tools to eliminate some of this misinformation and tell what really did happen that night." To investigate the sinking, a team of naval architects, oceanographers, recovery experts, microbial biologists, metallurgists, and historians—assembled by RMS Titanic and the Discovery Channel in conjunction with France's Ellipse

Research and recovery missions to the *Titanic* rely on the French deep-diving, three-passenger submersible *Nautile*, one of only six in the world that are capable of diving to 20,000 feet. This diagram depicts *Nautile*'s engineering and search capabilities. 1. Manipulator arms 2. Sampling basket 3. Jettisonable 230V batteries 4. Oxygen storage 5. Main propeller 6. Lateral thruster 7. Shot ballast tanks 8. Top hatch 9. Scanning sonar 10. Still and video cameras. Right: The crew of the French research vessel *Nadir* lowers *Nautile* into the North Atlantic during the 1996 expedition.

Programme—participated in the month-long 1996 research and recovery expedition, led by French Navy commander Paul-Henri (P.-H.) Nargeolet—IFREMER's expedition leader and former commander in charge of the French Navy's deep-sea diving program—and RMS Titanic president George Tulloch.

The mission team included David Livingstone, senior naval architect for the shipbuilders Harland and Wolff and the first person from the firm ever to view the wreck of the *Titanic*; Paul Matthias of Polaris Imaging located in Narragansett, Rhode Island, an expert in underwater imaging technology; William H. Garzke, Jr., senior naval architect at Gibbs and Cox and chairman of the Forensics Panel of the Society of Naval Architects and Marine Engineers, which investigates maritime disasters around the globe; and Dr. D. Roy Cullimore, applied microbiologist and director of the Regina Water Research Institute at the University of Regina in Saskatchewan, Canada. Other members of the expedition team included *Titanic* historians and authors John Eaton, Charles Haas, and Claes-Göran Wetterholm; biologist and *Titanic* author Dr. Charles Pellegrino; Dr. Stéphane Pennec, archaeologist and expert in metal conservation; Martine Plantec, a specialist in textile conservation; deep-ocean cinematographer Christian Petron; and cultural anthropologist Holger Van der Ley. In addition, a team of scientific experts on both sides of the Atlantic analyzed data from the expedition's findings and added further insights into the truth about the *Titanic*'s sinking.

▲

Mike Strong (left), leader of the vessel *Jim Kilabuk*, and RMS Titanic president George Tulloch (right) planned research and recovery strategies using a scale model of the *Titanic*'s wreck. Top and left: *Nautile* begins its 2.5-mile free fall to the ocean bottom.

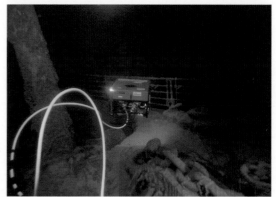

▲
The crew of the *Nautile* descending to the wreck site. Right: *Robin*, a remote-controlled robotic camera, can venture into areas that are too confined and dangerous for *Nautile*.

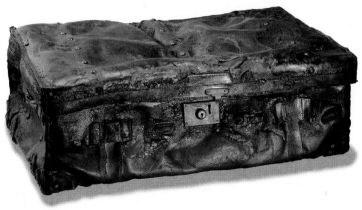

▲
Scientists have studied the *Titanic's* expansion joints, such as the one pictured above, to gain a clearer understanding of the disaster. Left: A suitcase with its lock still intact was recovered in 1987.

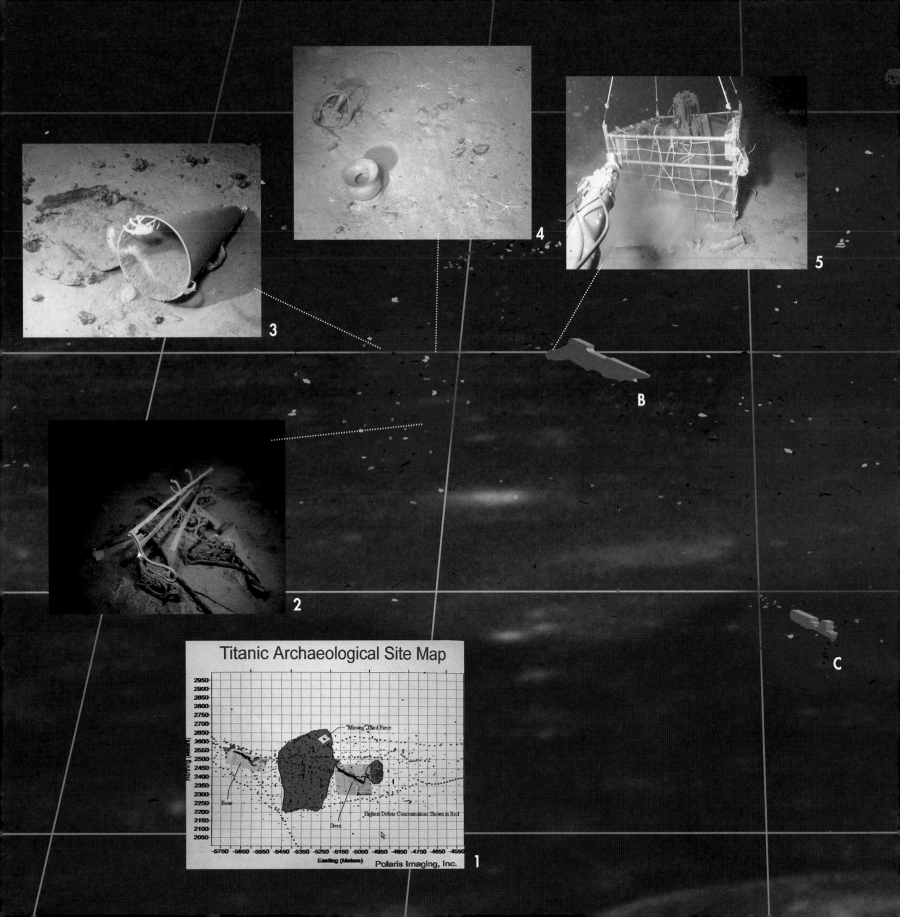

3

4

5

B

2

C

Titanic Archaeological Site Map

"Missing" Third Piece

Bow

Stern

Highest Debris Concentrations Shown in Red

Northing (Meters)

2950
2900
2850
2800
2750
2700
2650
2600
2550
2500
2450
2400
2350
2300
2250
2200
2150
2100
2050

-5750 -5650 -5550 -5450 -5350 -5250 -5150 -5050 -4950 -4850 -4750 -4650 -4550

Easting (Meters)

Polaris Imaging, Inc.

1

Sidescan sonar mounted on the Nautile submarine and EOSCAN—a data collection processing and display system—were used by Paul Matthias of Polaris Imaging during the 1996 expedition to compile a comprehensive Archaeological Site Map (1). The computer illustration of the map presented on this spread—which shows the site from the opposite position—depicts the locations of the bow (A), the stern (B), and the third piece (C). The illustration also shows the position of more than 400 pieces of debris, including a deck bench (2), a megaphone (3), a spittoon (4), the ship's compass (5), part of the winger bridge on the starboard side (6), the foremast navigational beacon (7), and a winch mechanism (8). The tinted areas of the map and computer illustration indicate areas that have a high concentration of debris.

▲

Sonar expert Paul Matthias attached acoustic equipment to *Nautile* to help him "see through the mud" burying the forward section of the *Titanic's* bow. His work revealed the long-hidden iceberg damage to the ship.

Revealing the *Titanic*'s Hidden Wounds

One of the most mysterious aspects of the *Titanic* disaster has been the nature of the wounds caused by the iceberg. Despite testimony buried in transcripts of the official inquiries held in 1912, it was commonly speculated and reported that the collision had inflicted a continuous 300-foot-long gash in the vessel's side. Perhaps the only person who could have answered the question definitively, however—Harland and Wolff's Thomas Andrews—had gone down with the *Titanic*, and the testimony of survivors was full of contradictions. There was, however, one expert at the 1912 British inquiry who believed he knew what had happened—a Harland and Wolff naval architect named Edward Wilding. Wilding asserted that it was not at all a huge gash that had sunk the ship; in fact, he believed the damage caused by the iceberg was extremely small. He based this conclusion on the reported pattern of the flooding and a study of the survivors' testimony. Since the ship flooded unevenly in six compartments, he determined that each compartment had suffered its own individual damage. If the iceberg did inflict a tear that was 300 feet long, he asserted that it could only have been three-quarters of an inch

wide to account for the rate of flooding. A gash as large and long as commonly assumed, he held, would have sunk the huge ship in a matter of minutes instead of hours. The press and the public, however, ignored Wilding's findings, and for nearly a century, people continued to believe that only an enormous, gaping gash could have doomed the immense liner.

Even after the *Titanic*'s wreck was found, the truth remained a mystery because most of the evidence of the iceberg's damage was buried under 45 feet of ocean-bottom mud. On the 1996 expedition, however, scientists hoped finally to reveal the truth. New sonar technology, used by geologists for seismic profiling, promised to "see through the mud" that covers the lower portions of the *Titanic*'s bow. To conduct the investigation, sonar expert Paul Matthias boarded IFREMER's deep-diving submersible *Nautile* to descend two and a half miles to the *Titanic*'s wreck. Equipped with nimble mechanical arms and packed with advanced electronic equipment, the $20-million *Nautile* is one of only six submersibles in the world capable of descending to 20,000 feet. For this investigation, *Nautile*'s mechanical arms were modified to carry a sub-bottom profiler capable of emitting low-frequency

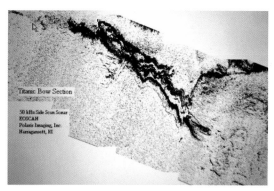

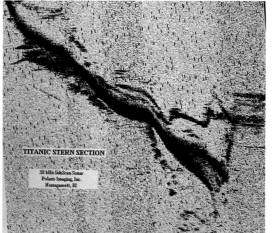

▲

EOSCAN and sidescan sonar mounted on the bottom of *Nautile* collected data to produce acoustic images much like medical ultrasound. The images shown here outline the *Titanic*'s stern (above), and the bow (top), both of which are buried deep in mud.

acoustic signals that would penetrate the seabed. This was the first time this technology would be used to image openings in a hull beneath the mud, and there was no guarantee of success. But on the pitch-black ocean bottom, as the signals moved through the seabed silt and the steel of the *Titanic*'s hull, they created an acoustic image of the long-hidden portions of the starboard bow, much like a medical ultrasound. Luck, it turned out, was on the team's side. During the three-hour survey, Matthias was at last able to "see" the iceberg holes that had been buried and debated for eighty-five years.

What the sonar imaging revealed was startling. The *Titanic*'s wound was not, in fact, a giant, gaping slash. Instead, it was a series of six thin slits, some only as wide as a human finger. The damage, incredibly, totaled no more than 12 square feet—about the size of a human body. Just as Edward Wilding had predicted, these tiny wounds created a pattern of flooding that led to the demise of the largest ship the world had ever known. "Wilding had no computers, no sonar images, no advanced technology of any kind," Charles Haas reflected, "yet he was able to virtually pinpoint the damage to the hull." Now that Wilding's theory had been confirmed by direct examination, expedition scientists turned to the next remaining mysteries. With such a small amount of damage, why did the *Titanic* sink so quickly? And could the tragedy have been prevented?

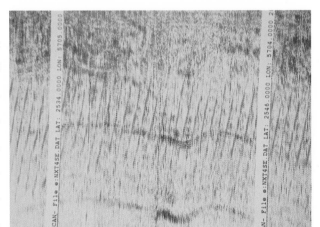

▲ Sonar imaging allowed this first look at the actual damage to the *Titanic*'s hull lying under the mud. Instead of the gaping gash, acoustic technology revealed six narrow openings caused by the *Titanic*'s collision with the iceberg. These openings, like the one shown above, were responsible for her sinking.

An inevitable disaster?

In Belfast, Northern Ireland, two Harland and Wolff naval architects, John Bedford and Chris Hackett, used a unique computer model that they and other Harland and Wolff engineers developed to recreate and analyze the sinking. Their goal was to investigate why such minor damage had caused the immense *Titanic* to sink in just under three hours. The model mathematically confirmed the inevitable, tragic sequence of events that Wilding had deduced in 1912. Bedford and Hackett calculated that immediately after the *Titanic* struck the iceberg at 11:40 P.M., water rushed into her hull at a powerful rate of almost 7 tons per second. Although the holes in the liner's side were small, they were located 20 feet below the waterline, where high pressure would have rapidly forced the sea through the narrow slits faster than water through a fire hose. Just ten minutes after the collision, most of the damaged compartments were already flooded to the top. By midnight, the engineers calculated, the *Titanic* had taken on 7,450 tons of water and began plunging by the bow. By 12:40 A.M., only an hour after impact, they estimated that she had taken on 25,000 tons of water. By 2:00, she was flooded with 39,000 tons, forcing her bow underwater and heaving her stern up into the sky. A combination of high water pressure and 12 square feet of damage sank the largest, safest liner in the world.

Could the *Titanic*'s tragedy have been prevented? The engineers used their computer model to explore different hypothetical scenarios. If the *Titanic* had struck the iceberg head on instead of grazing it along her side, they determined, the ship might actually have survived—as Edward Wilding, once again, correctly asserted in 1912. In a head-on crash, the first 100 feet of the bow would have crumpled like an accordion, surely killing a number of passengers and crew members, but the *Titanic* most likely would have stayed afloat. What if the watertight doors had been left open so that the flooding would have been evenly distributed? That decision, they concluded, would have proved totally disastrous for the ship and her passengers. With the doors open, all the boiler and engine rooms would have flooded, causing the ship to lose its power and lights, and the *Titanic* would have capsized before all the lifeboats could have been launched. Aside from crashing into the iceberg head on, there is one decision that most probably would have saved the liner: slowing down. If the *Titanic* had prudently steamed half as fast as her 22.5-knot speed, according to naval architect Bill Garzke, she would have suffered far less damage, and fewer of her compartments would have flooded. The *Titanic* would have been injured, but she would likely have completed her maiden voyage to New York. To the credit of the *Titanic*'s designers, however, the liner remained afloat for two hours and forty minutes—long enough for nearly all the lifeboats to be launched. By contrast, Cunard's great liner *Lusitania* sank in less than twenty minutes after it was torpedoed by a German submarine in 1915, a disaster that resulted in the deaths of 1,198 passengers and crew.

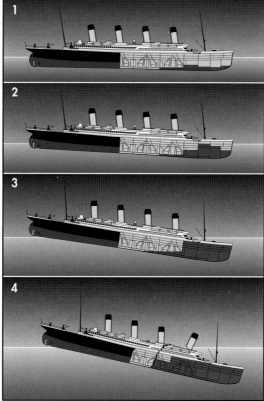

1. Six different wounds resulted in uneven flooding at a rate of 7 tons per second. 2. Water rose in the ship's fore compartments as the forward bulkhead of boiler room 5 collapsed. 3. Flooding was still confined, but almost 31,000 tons of water had been taken on.
4. Water from boiler room 5 began to spill into boiler room 4, driving the bow down and greatly straining the midsection. Around 2 A.M. the steel structure of the ship began to tear apart.

* * *

When and how did the *Titanic* split in two?

Until the *Titanic*'s wreck was discovered and explored, it was widely assumed that she had plunged to the ocean bottom in one piece, based on the testimony of all of the surviving ship's officers during the U.S. and British inquiries. A handful of survivors, however, contradicted those accounts, claiming that the ship had split apart before sinking. They described how, in the final moments, the *Titanic*'s stern had heaved upright into the air, the forward funnel had crashed into the water from the strain, and the ship had begun to come apart. "There are almost as many interpretations and depictions of the breakup as there are people who have testimony," noted *Titanic* historian John Eaton. Although some survivors claimed the ship broke apart underwater, the young survivor Jack Thayer insisted that the *Titanic* split before sinking, even going so far as to have a sketch made and published that clearly depicted the *Titanic* breaking in two pieces at the surface.

To uncover the truth about the breakup of the ship, Bill Garzke's colleagues at Gibbs and Cox in Arlington, Virginia, constructed a virtual *Titanic* through computer modeling, based on new metallurgical information resulting from the 1996 expedition, computer analysis by Bedford and Hackett, and some of the *Titanic*'s design plans. Using this data, engineers, for the first time, were able to begin calculating the stresses that acted on the great ship's hull before the *Titanic* began to break apart. What the engineers discovered is that the *Titanic* actually began bending on the ocean surface. As the stresses on her midsection increased, the steel plates in her keel began to compress and buckle, her decks began to fold down, and the great ship's hull began to shatter. As her bow pulled down, her huge stern rose in the air, towering as high as a fifteen-story building over the water. The resulting pressure on the deck was greater than 35,000

▲

Naval architects David Livingstone (left) of Harland and Wolff and William Garzke of Gibbs and Cox studied the *Titanic*'s plans and construction documentation to help formulate answers to some of the questions that have perplexed *Titanic* historians for decades.

pounds per square inch, well above her capacity of 22,400 pounds per square inch—stresses so enormous that they overwhelmed the ship, and she began to break apart.

Contributing to the breakup, Garzke believes, was the quality of the steel used in the *Titanic*'s construction. "Brittle steel" was a common problem plaguing turn-of-the-century ships. Although ore quality and processing techniques varied widely, steel produced at the time the *Titanic* was built generally had a higher percentage of sulfur and phosphorous than would be permissible today, resulting in steel that fractured easily. In one case, in fact, an entire ship was known to have split in half without crashing into anything. On the night of the *Titanic* disaster, many survivors claimed they heard awful and frightening sounds. According to Garzke, it is possible that the noises heard that night were the *Titanic*'s steel plates shattering like glass.

To find out, more than 200 pounds of mangled, rusted steel from the *Titanic*'s debris field—hull plates, beams, and a bit of bulkhead—were brought to the surface during the 1996 expedition, after nearly a century at the deep bottom of the ocean. Garzke and Livingstone spent hours examining the fragments. The samples were then sent to the United States for a battery of tests to determine the steel's chemical makeup, tensile strength, microstructure,

▲

David Livingstone (left), IFREMER's Paul-Henri (P.-H.) Nargeolet (center), and William Garzke (right) review video footage of one of the *Nautile*'s daily dives to the *Titanic* site. The *Nautile* extensively photographed the fragmented hull and debris field during the 1996 expedition.

The Sinking and Breakup of the *Titanic*

New scientific evidence has shed light on the sequence of events that led to the breakup and final sinking of the *Titanic* on April 14-15, 1912.

1. The ship's collision with the iceberg at 11:40 P.M. did not tear a 300-foot gash along her side, as the public had long assumed, but caused only glancing damage—a series of six thin slits, some only as wide as a human finger, that totaled a mere 12 square feet. Immediately after the collision, water rushed into the *Titanic*'s hull at the rate of almost 7 tons per second. Although the holes in the liner's side were small, they were located 20 feet below the waterline, where high pressure would have rapidly forced the sea through the narrow slits faster than water through a fire hose. By 12:40 A.M., only an hour after impact, the *Titanic* had taken on 25,000 tons of water and was sinking at the bow.

2. By 2:00 A.M., the *Titanic* was flooded with 39,000 tons of water, forcing her bow underwater. As the stresses on her midsection increased, the ship began bending on the ocean surface. The steel plates in her keel began to compress and buckle, her decks began to fold down, her forward funnel collapsed, and her hull began to shatter.

5. After the *Titanic* broke apart, the stern rotated on the surface, then remained nearly vertical for at least a minute, while the bow and the small "third piece" sank toward the bottom of the sea.

8. The *Titanic*'s stern section was filled with air at the surface. As the stern sank, pressure increased on the trapped air, causing the stern section to implode.

9. The implosion and the shock of impact on the seabed left the stern section a tangled mass of twisted steel, resting 2,000 feet from the bow section on the ocean bottom.

3. Some survivors recalled that the *Titanic*'s stern had heaved into the air, the forward funnel had crashed into the water, and the ship had begun to come apart on the surface. New computer modeling of the disaster has demonstrated that as the *Titanic*'s stern rose, the resulting pressure on the deck was greater than 35,000 pounds per square inch, well above her capacity of 22,400 pounds per square inch—stresses so huge that they caused the ship to break apart.

4. The quality of the *Titanic*'s steel may have contributed to the breakup. Much of the steel produced in 1912 contained high levels of sulfur and phosphorous and fractured easily. New testing has shown that this "brittle steel" loses strength in water that is 28°F, the temperature of the North Atlantic on the night the *Titanic* sank. The horrendous noise that survivors heard shortly before the ship sank may have been the sound of the *Titanic*'s steel shattering as the ship broke into three main pieces.

6. Since the *Titanic*'s bow was already flooded with water on the surface, it was not crushed by the increasing water pressure as it sank. The bow plummeted toward the bottom at 30 miles an hour or more. As it plunged, thousands of objects—including pieces of heavy machinery as well as china, silverware, suitcases, and furniture—scattered across the seabed, creating a debris field between the bow and stern sections.

7. The front end of the bow slammed into the seabed, burying itself in 45 feet of silt. The back end of the bow then abruptly smashed up against the front end, bending the hull from the impact.

and grain size, as well as its responses to low temperatures. At the University of Missouri in Rolla, metallurgist Professor H. P. Leighley guided a team that tested the *Titanic*'s steel to see if it was brittle. After cutting a small sample and loading it into a scanning electron microscope, metallurgists Chris Ramsey and Scott Miller peered deep into the steel's microstructure to look for potential weaknesses and defects in the steel. As they suspected, the steel was full of large manganese sulfide inclusions—chemical imperfections that create weak areas, causing the metal to be brittle. At the time the *Titanic* was built, no one suspected that these chemical impurities could make steel fragile under extreme conditions—such as the unusually cold, 28°F water temperature of the North Atlantic on April 14 and 15, 1912.

To test the steel's response to water that cold, Professor Leighley chilled a bar of *Titanic* steel to 28°F, then subjected it to violent impact. The steel immediately fractured. To confirm the findings, the fractured sample of *Titanic* steel was then sent to a laboratory at the National Institute of Standards & Technology in Gaithersburg, Maryland. There, materials scientist Timothy Foecke confirmed that the metal became more brittle when subjected to such frigid temperatures. In almost every case, Foecke found, the fracture lines traced back to weak spots in the steel, confirming the disastrous effect of imperfec-

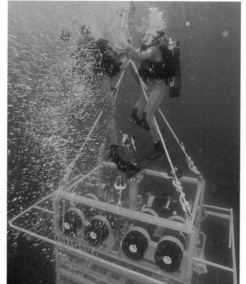

▲

In 1996, exploration on the pitch-black ocean floor was aided by the most powerful illumination of the *Titanic* ever achieved. Four truck-size light towers were lowered to the wreck site, each holding five 1,200-watt, battery-powered haloid metallic iodide (HMI) floodlights. The towers illuminated the wreck site with lighting equivalent to 35,000 household bulbs.

tions in the metal. "More or less," the scientist explained, "when you take the steel down to a lower temperature, you're actually shattering something that's full of holes." The night of the disaster—as a result of enormous stress, cold temperatures, and imperfections in the steel—the *Titanic*'s hull may simply have shattered like glass on the ocean surface. "Metallurgical testing," Garzke concluded, "has shown that brittle steel at those cold North Atlantic water temperatures indeed lost all of its strength, contributing to the breakup of the *Titanic*—although we'll never be 100 percent certain of what happened." Even decades later, brittle steel led to the hull fractures of World War II Liberty ships and T-2 tankers; it was not until 1947 that the phenomenon was recognized and that the composition of ships' steel was strictly regulated.

* * *

The journey to the bottom

Nobody is certain what happened to the *Titanic* once she dipped beneath the waves and plunged to the ocean floor. The ship's bow and stern portions somehow came to rest 2,000 feet apart on the sea bottom, in dramatically different conditions. The hull is relatively intact, while the stern section is mangled almost beyond recognition. What happened to the *Titanic*'s hull and stern as they sank to the bottom of the sea?

To investigate this question, Harland and

The *Titanic*'s stern section, unlike the relatively intact bow, is an almost unrecognizable mass of tangled, twisted steel. The two sections lie 2,000 feet apart on the seabed, facing in opposite directions.

A rusticle-encrusted cylinder head, a part of one of the *Titanic*'s giant, four-story reciprocating engines, appears out of the darkness. Left: A silver plate recovered from the *Titanic*'s debris field.

Wolff's David Livingstone dove to the wreck aboard *Nautile* and inspected the mangled scrap heap of the stern section during the August 1996 expedition. His view was aided by the most powerful illumination of the wreck ever achieved. Four truck-size light towers, weighing 3 tons each and constructed at a cost of a million dollars, were lowered to the wreck site, each holding five 1,200-watt, battery-powered haloid metallic iodide (HMI) floodlights. Their quartz bulbs generated light power equivalent to 35,000 household bulbs and were capable of withstanding pressures greater than 8,000 pounds per square inch. The effect on the ocean bottom was "incredible," Livingstone said. "It's not quite like being in a [lighted] stadium, but they make a fantastic difference." Never before was so much light cast on the *Titanic* or on any other object in the deep ocean. What Livingstone saw was a stern section damaged so extensively that "It looks like the whole lot has been picked up, shaken, and dropped. . . . There's no pattern" to the damage, he explained. "You see pipes in good shape with their flanges still intact right next to pipes that are completely smashed." Livingstone also noticed that one of the huge, four-and-a-half-story, 990-ton engines seemed to have snapped in half, evidence of the immense forces that were acting on the hull during the sinking. He also examined a giant, 60-degree bend below the bridge on the port side of the bow, an immense deformation that was first observed during the 1996 expedition.

Back on the surface, Livingstone and Garzke attempted to reconstruct what happened to the bow and stern once they had slipped beneath the water. They believed that since the bow was already flooded with water on the surface, it was not crushed by increasing water pressure as it sank. The bend he saw in the bow, Livingstone noted, could be a clue to what happened on the bottom. The plates of the bow section may have buckled while the *Titanic* sank, he speculated. Then when the forward part of the bow abruptly hit the seabed, the back end may have smashed into the forward section, bending the hull like a concertina from the impact.

Understanding how the stern arrived at the bottom is more puzzling. The chaotic nature of the stern wreckage is an important clue. Livingstone and Garzke theorized that after the bow pulled the stern underwater, the two halves separated. As the stern section sank, the immense water pressure on the air trapped inside the stern caused it to implode. Livingstone concluded that the aft end of the stern then hit the bottom first, since the propellers are curiously bent upward. Anything that was not well attached to the stern's hull probably broke loose from the shock of impact.

▲

During the sinking, tremendous stresses on the steel plates of the *Titanic*'s hull may have caused the deafening noises reported by survivors. Scientists believe that sea water that filled the bow saved it from being crushed by increasing water pressure as the ship sank.

The final chapter

Since the *Titanic*'s wreck was discovered in 1985, another fact has become clear. The *Titanic* is disintegrating rapidly, as its hull is being steadily consumed by rust. How fast the ship is corroding, however, remains a mystery. To answer that question, Canadian microbial ecologist Dr. Roy D. Cullimore joined the 1996 *Titanic* expedition. His mission was to determine what types of bacteria and other biological life have colonized the *Titanic*'s hull and to analyze the wreck's rate of decomposition and erosion. Cullimore is an expert on "rusticles," the elaborate, iron-rich structures that cover most of the exposed surfaces of the hull. The rusticles are formed by microbes that remove iron from the ship, and Cullimore has concluded that they are the main culprits destroying the *Titanic* as she rests on the seabed. "The ship is disintegrating," he explained, "because the rusticles are sucking more and more iron out of the steel." As a result, he predicted, "the integrity, the structure of the ship, will one day collapse."

To aid his investigation, plastic containers holding specially prepared tubes were placed by *Nautile* on the bow of the *Titanic*, where they remained for two weeks. Each of the tubes contained a plastic pipe wrapped in gauze, a short strip of color slide film, and a blend of nutrients and iron salts that served as bait for microbes. *Nautile* later carefully collected a variety of rusticle structures from different parts of the wreck for Cullimore's analysis. After two weeks, the submersible brought the tubes back to the surface. Bacterial colonies from the rusticles growing on the ship's hull had worked their way inside, consuming the protein emulsion on the film. Back in his mobile lab aboard the research vessel *Ocean Voyager*, Cullimore then studied the contaminated film strips, which revealed colorful traces caused by bacterial digestion of the film. According to Cullimore, these etchings are signs of a vigorous community of life on the *Titanic*. "It's a complicated living system, and it's not just one species," he explained. The shell of the rusticles also hosts numerous organisms; Cullimore has found them to be inhabited by bacteria and molds, and he plans to culture them to learn how they grow in these fragile, iron-rich shells. One of the most fascinating findings about rusticles, he added, is their immense complexity. They embody a web of water channels, ducts, and cavities, and a vast amount of surface area. "If I took sixty-five tons of rusticles from the bow of the *Titanic* and spread their surfaces out," he stated, "it would cover 23,000 square miles." Essentially, he added, rusticles are highly complex communities; "we don't understand all of the components. This is a new part of science that we're just starting to explore—the edge of yet another universe."

To find answers to the final question—how much time the *Titanic* may have left—Cullimore has extracted some of the ship's iron each time he has analyzed a sample of rusticle. Judging from the amount of iron he has collected, he determined that as much as half of the bow plating in places has already been consumed by these iron-eating bacteria. As the ship continues to lose iron to the rusticles, it will, sooner rather than later, collapse in on itself. Eventually, the *Titanic* will turn to dust on the ocean floor.

▲

Elaborate, iron-rich structures called "rusticles" cover most of the exposed surfaces of the *Titanic*'s hull. Immensely complex, they contain vast labyrinths of water channels, ducts, and cavities. A single ton of rusticles with all its surfaces spread out would cover more than 350 square miles.

In his lab on the research vessel *Ocean Voyager*, Dr. D. Roy Cullimore, applied microbiologist at the University of Regina in Saskatchewan, Canada, examines biological sampling tubes placed on the *Titanic*.

Rusticles form numerous structures, including hanging growths, flat plates, and spikelike formations. Formed by microbes, the rusticles are removing iron from the ship and will gradually destroy the *Titanic*, causing her to be recycled into the ocean environment. Cullimore's objective in 1996 was to identify the iron-eating bacteria and to calculate the rate at which the *Titanic* is disintegrating.

THE TRAIL OF TIME

TIME DOES NOT STAND still on the sea bottom. The wreck of the *Titanic* is dissolving into dust, with no possibility of rescue. And the trail of artifacts strewn across the Atlantic floor—all that physically remains of her passengers and crew—is also doomed to disappear in the hostile environment of the ocean. If not recovered, these pieces of history will be consumed by bacteria, corroded by salt and acids, and abraded by sediments until they are recycled into the vast Atlantic, reduced to mere stains on the seabed.

From the beginning, however, efforts to rescue these tangible objects of memory—from clocks and cooking pots to the ship's great whistles and the large bell from the base of the ship's foremast—have been met

▲

This gold wristwatch, found in good condition, was recovered in 1987 with other valuables. Left: The French submarine *Jules* is used to assist the expedition team with jobs close to the surface.

with protests from a few who wish to leave the *Titanic*'s wreck site undisturbed as a memorial. Charges of grave robbing have been hurled at those who believe the objects are historically important and should be saved, conserved, and displayed for the public before the sea destroys them.

One critic has declared that it isn't "necessary to plunder [the *Titanic*'s] grave site, open wounds in some of the affected families, or stir [up] controversy" since, he noted, "we are not talking about discovering ancient civilizations or preserving history from an unknown era." Those on the other side of the issue, however, have argued that charges of grave robbing have never been applied to the gathering of artifacts from other shipwrecks—and that the immense variety of objects scattered across the sea floor are an integral part of the *Titanic*'s story. "The scientific recovery and educational display of *Titanic* artifacts will broaden our knowledge of this magnificent ship, her passengers and crew, and the tragedy of her sinking, which continues to generate world-wide interest," countered Robert M. DiSogra, president of Titanic International. "The world wasn't black and white in 1912, and we shouldn't have to limit our understanding of the ship to historic photographs. Nothing is more compelling than seeing *Titanic* artifacts in three dimensions." Swedish *Titanic* historian Claes-Göran Wetterholm agrees. "If you want to get in close contact with history," he explained, "you can't just read about it. You have to have artifacts, a three-dimensional insight into history. That's something that's clearly understood by every museum in the world." Many people believe that seeing and touching the artifacts brings the human dimension of the tragedy to life—and that the objects, carefully conserved and exhibited to the public, will preserve the *Titanic*'s memory long after the survivors and the ship itself are gone.

Despite the controversy, thousands of objects have been painstakingly recovered from the *Titanic*'s debris field since 1987 by an international archaeological collaboration between

▲

RMS Titanic's George Tulloch (left) and IFREMER's P.-H. Nargeolet (right), former commander of the French Navy's deep-sea diving program, have organized four international research and recovery missions to the *Titanic*. Nargeolet has made more dives to the *Titanic*'s wreck than any other individual in the world.

RMS Titanic, Inc., and IFREMER, the French oceanographic institute. From the beginning, New York–based RMS Titanic has pledged to recover and conserve the artifacts to the highest technical, archaeological, and museum standards and to maintain them in a permanent collection that will be displayed to the public around the world. None of the objects will ever be offered for private sale. Due in part to that commitment, RMS Titanic was granted guardianship rights to the wreck by a United States Federal court order in 1994, under the ancient common laws of marine salvage. In order to safeguard the *Titanic* and ensure that her artifacts are conserved and exhibited to the highest archaeological standards, RMS Titanic has joined with Great Britain's National Maritime Museum to create the Titanic International Advisory Committee, whose members include representatives from *Titanic* historical societies as well as European and American maritime museums. "The whole museum community," explained Dr. Eric Kentley, chief curator of Britain's National Maritime Museum, "is concerned that these objects are kept together in a secure way, that they're brought up responsibly, that they're adequately documented, adequately conserved and, ultimately, go on public exhibition."

▲

The French research vessel *Nadir* has been the command ship for four *Titanic* missions. Right: Artifacts including this shoe brush, perhaps once used by stewards to polish passengers' shoes, have been found in remarkable condition.

THE PHYSICAL PROCESS OF retrieving artifacts from the deep bottom of the ocean, however, is a dangerous, expensive proposition that pushes the limits of late-twentieth-century engineering and technology. According to expedition leader P.-H. Nargeolet of IFREMER, who also worked on the 1985 French-American team that discovered the *Titanic*, the bottom of the Atlantic Ocean is "the most hostile environment known to man. Descending to those depths, with those immense pressures, presents a technical challenge that surpasses the challenge of traveling into space, with its absence of pressure. That's why mankind walked on the moon almost two decades before we were able to perform work at the bottom of the ocean."

All of the *Titanic* recovery missions have relied on the advanced capabilities of IFREMER's deep-diving submersible *Nautile*, which has completed ninety-six successful dives to the wreck site—a record equivalent to spending six months at the bottom of the sea. After free-falling two and a half miles to the ocean floor, where pressures are comparable to those beneath the Space Shuttle's engines at blast-off, *Nautile* spends hours on the seabed gently retrieving artifacts with its two nimble robotic arms, manipulated by the pilot. Equipped with scooping, grasping, and IFREMER's

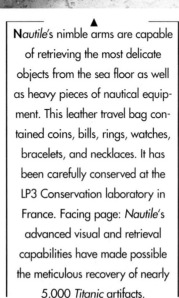

Nautile's nimble arms are capable of retrieving the most delicate objects from the sea floor as well as heavy pieces of nautical equipment. This leather travel bag contained coins, bills, rings, watches, bracelets, and necklaces. It has been carefully conserved at the LP3 Conservation laboratory in France. Facing page: *Nautile*'s advanced visual and retrieval capabilities have made possible the meticulous recovery of nearly 5,000 *Titanic* artifacts.

patented vacuum suction devices, *Nautile*'s arms are capable of collecting small, fragile artifacts such as teacups and glass bowls as well as massive, heavy pieces of nautical equipment, such as the *Titanic*'s massive bitts and lifeboat davits. Once *Nautile* carefully lifts objects from the seabed, its robotic arms place the artifacts into a retractable basket it carries in front of the craft or into wire cages, lined with syntactic foam, that have been lowered to the ocean bottom from the mother ship *Nadir*.

On the first recovery mission, in the summer of 1987, *Nautile* retrieved some eighteen hundred objects in thirty-two dives to the *Titanic*'s vast debris field. The extensive array of *Titanic* relics recovered on this mission included a gilded chandelier; the compass, wheel pedestal, and two telegraphs from the ship's stern docking bridge; one of the ship's bells; a porthole; a bronze cherub; and a pristine window made of leaded glass. Technicians who descended aboard *Nautile* on this first retrieval expedition were astounded by the remarkable condition of many of the objects that they found. Solid silver, brass, and copper serving pieces looked as though they had just been polished by a scullery maid, and 238 pristine au gratin dishes were found stacked just as they had been arranged in 1912 inside a wooden crate that had long since crumbled into dust.

To raise massive nautical equipment such as a 3-ton bitt—used for securing cables on the *Titanic*—*Nadir*'s crew members lower lifting bags to the ocean bottom, using heavy chain as ballast. They then rig the lift bags to the artifact. When the ballast is removed, the bags float the object to the surface.

Crew members fill the lift bags with lighter-than-water diesel fuel, which is later pumped back into the *Nadir*'s fuel supply.

In June 1993, a second RMS Titanic expedition completed fifteen 8-to-12-hour dives and retrieved eight hundred additional artifacts—many of exceptional historical interest, including one of the ship's great whistles, a double lifeboat davit, and part of the liner's giant reciprocating engine. On this mission, technicians also explored the hull of the *Titanic* with *Robin*, a remote-controlled robotic camera capable of venturing into areas that are too confined and dangerous for *Nautile*. *Robin* explored the grand staircase with its ghostly chandeliers and peered through a great gash in the *Titanic*'s side into the liner's mail-sorting room, where sacks of undelivered letters have rested since April 1912. The following summer, *Nautile* completed eighteen more dives to the wreck, retrieving fragile relics that included a camera, a gold pocket watch, souvenir plates from Holland, and a passenger's binoculars. On this mission, the team also recovered an immense piece of equipment from the ship—a massive, 3-ton bitt to which the liner's mooring lines were once attached. To raise the giant piece of metal, *Nautile* fastened a wire cable around it, then attached it to lifting bags filled with lighter-than-water diesel fuel, which floated the enormous bitt two and a half miles up to the surface.

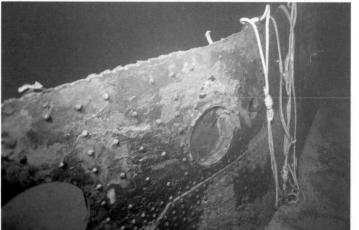

▲

Although the 1996 expedition team attempted to raise a huge section of hull plating that was situated some 70 feet east of the stern wreckage (previous spread and above), bad weather hindered recovery attempts. The team managed to float the piece within 215 feet of the surface, but the nylon ropes holding it snapped one by one in violent seas, and the piece floated back down to the sea bottom. It landed, upright in the mud, 10 miles from its original position.

In August 1996, the RMS Titanic–IFREMER team attempted to recover an even bigger relic—an amidships section of the *Titanic*'s hull, 14 feet wide and 23.5 feet long, that was lying in the debris field. Situated some 70 feet east of the stern wreckage, the piece had been discovered in 1993 and closely examined and measured in 1994. According to Harland and Wolff's David Livingstone and historian John Eaton, the boot-shaped slab formed part of the outer wall of two first-class berths—unoccupied cabins C79 and C81, which were located next to the cabin occupied by W. T. Stead, the renowned British journalist. The weight of the piece, more than three stories high and two stories wide, was estimated to be about 22 tons. To retrieve the huge section of hull plating, *Nautile*'s crew rigged it with cables and steel rings, then connected the cables to lift bags that would, they hoped, raise the hull section to the surface. The piece would then be winched onto a recovery ship—the *Jim Kilabuk*, a supply vessel sailing from St. Johns, Newfoundland—to be transported to North America for restoration and exhibition. Unfortunately, bad weather plagued the recovery attempts. Although the team eventually raised the piece to within 215 feet of the surface, the nylon ropes holding it snapped one by

Dr. Stéphane Pennec of LP3 Conservation in France studies the amount of corrosion on the *Titanic*'s bitts. Left: Another set of bitts remains unrecovered in the murky waters of the ocean bottom.

one in violent, 12- to 14-foot waves, and the hull piece floated back down to the sea bottom—where it landed, embedded upright in the mud, 10 miles from the *Titanic*'s wreck, with six of its eight lift bags still attached. "The ocean gives no quarter," reflected expedition leader George Tulloch. "We failed on this attempt because we neglected to carefully coordinate the twenty-first-century technology of deep ocean recovery with the nineteenth-century technology of winching and rigging. We won't make that mistake again."

* * *

RMS TITANIC STILL HOPES the large hull piece will one day be the centerpiece of the publicly displayed *Titanic* artifact collection. Nearly five thousand smaller *Titanic* objects have, however, been successfully recovered from the sea—and the challenge of preserving them is expanding the limits of deep-ocean archaeology and conservation science. The objects—ranging from clothing and metal ship's fittings to leather suitcases and porcelain bowls—are among the only artifacts in the world ever recovered from such tremendous depths, near the abyssal zone of the Atlantic Ocean. Conservators and archaeologists know very little about what happens to different materials in this extraordinary environment. "It's the first time," said Dr. Stéphane Pennec of Atelier LP3

▲

Dr. Stéphane Pennec (left) and Martine Plantec (right) carefully repack the contents of a recovered suitcase—clothing, gloves, and a suit—in order to stabilize them before treatment. Left: These recovered chandeliers are are immediately placed in water aboard ship until they can be treated in the lab.

Conservation in France, "that we have had to deal with artifacts that have been in water so deep and so long." Most shipwreck recovery efforts take place in much shallower water, where objects have been subjected to less pressure and more light. At the depth of the *Titanic*, however, there is no light at all, hardly any oxygen, near-freezing temperatures, acidic bottom silt, and pressure 400 times greater than the atmosphere—pressure high enough to push corks into wine bottles and crush the hollow handles of forks and spoons. Deep-sea microorganisms that metabolize metal have stained artifacts with black sulfides. The electrochemical activity of sea water has corroded many metal objects, especially those made of iron and copper. And under the sea, the fibers of organic materials break apart and decompose, making them extremely weak and porous.

All recovered objects must be treated immediately after they are exposed to air, or many would quickly start to crumble. Salts embedded in ceramics, for example, can crystallize and rupture delicate glazes. And the surface of retrieved metal objects, especially those made of iron, can explode, fizzling and steaming, when exposed to oxygen in air. Wood, leather, paper, and other organic objects can also deteriorate quickly if allowed to dry, since bacteria and fungi grow more quickly when these materials are exposed to oxygen, and their long-saturated fibers can lose their shape. As a result, all artifacts are immediately stabilized as soon as they are brought up to the surface. After careful cleaning with a soft brush, they are placed in foam-lined tubs of water on the ship and documented with detailed measurements, condition reports, and photographs before transfer to an on-shore conservation laboratory.

The research laboratory at Electricité de France (EDF) was chosen to restore objects from the first RMS Titanic expedition. Because of the vast number of artifacts recovered since 1987, all other objects have been treated at LP3 Conservation, one of EDF's affiliated independent laboratories. Located in Burgundy, LP3 performs most of its work for museums and private collections. There, Dr. Pennec—archaeologist and former director of the EDF research lab—and Dr. Martine Plantec head a team of specialists in marine archaeology, ethnographic materials, metals, textiles, wood, and paper. Conservators at LP3 take a minimalist approach to restoration—removing corrosion and restoring the items to their appearance upon discovery—in the belief that the objects convey more meaning and reality if they display the effects of the traumas they have suffered.

As soon as the objects are received

At LP3 Conservation in Burgundy, France, an expert in paper restoration painstakingly cleans a deck of cards belonging to Howard Irwin. The playing cards were recovered during an expedition to the wreck site in 1993.

by the lab, they are washed repeatedly in deionized water to leach out contaminating surface salts. Artifacts are then treated to remove salts and other potentially damaging impurities that have accumulated deep inside the material. Electrolysis can be particularly effective for restoring metal objects, from an aluminum megaphone that may have been used by Captain Smith to the intricate sand-cast bronze supports that once adorned a deck bench. Since sea water conducts electricity, metal objects soaked in the ocean conduct a tiny current, causing negative ions from dissolved salts to attack uneven surfaces of the metal, such as seams and cracks. Although some metallic artifacts are too decayed to save—particularly those that are made of less dense substances or a combination of several metals—conservators can often partly reverse the corrosion process by placing the metal objects in chemical baths, wiring them to a negative battery terminal, and covering them with a metal cage connected to a positive terminal. The current pulls the negative ions and salt out of the artifact, effectively removing the corrosion.

Scientists working with the *Titanic* artifacts have also found that electric currents can remove salts from paper, leather, and wood as well. These materials are also

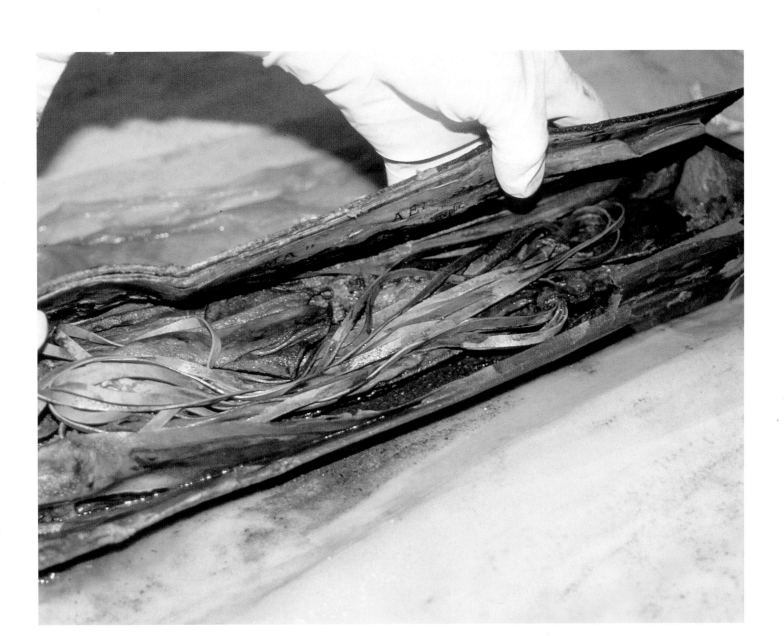

Sulfides have blackened this artifact, a child's wooden model "aeroplane" kit complete with instructions and rubberbands for a wind-up propeller. Left: A silver plate, bearing the White Star Line logo, after treatment.

treated with chemical agents to remove rust and fumigated if they appear to be contaminated by mold. In addition, polyethylene glycol, a water-soluble wax, can be injected into organic objects such as wood and leather to fill the spaces left by water as they dry. Conservators are treating an astonishing array of organic materials that have survived more than eight decades on the North Atlantic floor. Entire suitcases have been recovered, with trousers, shirts, and gloves still packed inside. The greatest *Titanic* treasure, however, is the immense amount of paper recovered from the wreck, from sheets of music to personal letters and bank notes. These discoveries, and their remarkably good condition, have amazed conservators. "It's unbelievable," Pennec said. "Nobody would have thought that paper could have been recovered" after more than eighty years at the bottom of the ocean. Most of the materials were protected from decomposition because they were stored inside leather bags, and many can be made fully readable again through newly developed conservation techniques. Papers are first freeze-dried to remove all water. They are then treated to protect them against mold and resized to restore their shape. All recovered artifacts are carefully maintained in an environment of controlled temperature and humidity and kept away from sunlight. Historians are also consulted to help identify the artifacts, which become a vital part of the *Titanic*'s ongoing historical record.

Hundreds of the *Titanic*'s relics have been conserved and are now being exhibited around the world. Displays in France, Norway, and Sweden have been followed by major exhibitions at the National Maritime Museum in Greenwich, England—an event that drew more than 700,000 people, the largest exhibition attendance in the history of the museum—as well as in Memphis, Tennessee, and Hamburg, Germany. Subsequent exhibitions of *Titanic* artifacts will travel to cities throughout North America and Europe. Ultimately, RMS Titanic hopes to construct a permanent home for the collection. Before that, plans are to launch a waterborne exhibit that can carry these fragile objects around the world —providing a physical connection with one of the most compelling tragedies of all time and keeping the memory and legacy of the *Titanic* and her lost passengers and crew members alive.

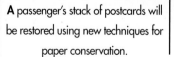

▲
A passenger's stack of postcards will be restored using new techniques for paper conservation.

CARTE POSTALE

▲

A conservator carefully separates this stack of postcards after freeze-drying the paper to remove all moisture. Left: A recovered Italian glazed pot displaying the White Star logo.

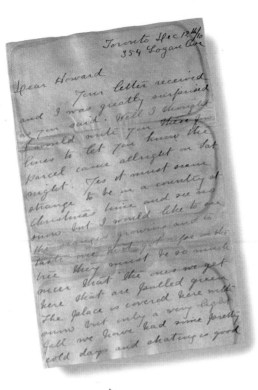

▲ **B**ank of England £5 note.

▲ **B**usiness card.

JOHN MITCHELL, JR. CO. INC.
STEAM, GAS & WATER SUPPLIES

JAMES A. MESSER
VICE-PRES. & GENL. MGR.

▲

A letter found in a bag belonging to Howard Irwin, who may have been a passenger under an assumed name after traveling to Australia and other parts of the globe. It was from a Mrs. Shuttle—the mother of Pearl Shuttle, a Canadian variety-show performer who was Irwin's girlfriend. Mrs. Shuttle's letter reads in part: "Yes, it must seem strange to be in a country at Christmas time and see no snow but I would like to see the oranges growing and to taste one that got ripe on the tree they must be so much nicer than the ones we get here that are pulled green. . . . Hoping you will have a pleasant time on Christmas and New Year . . . and I wish you prosperity wherever you go. Yours sincerely, Mrs. Shuttle."

▲ **S**econd-class luggage tag.

Dinner check. ▶

▲

This stock certificate, belonging to Franz Pulbaum, was for shares in an "amusement device" company.

Passenger's post card. ▼

◀ **A** $5 note from the California National Bank.

Silver-plated serving tray. ▼

▲ Bronze cherub that probably adorned the aft first-class grand staircase entrance at A deck.

A nickel saucepan. ▶

▼ **D**oor handle, possibly from a galley freezer.

▼ **B**rass spitoon bearing the White Star Line logo.

▼ **C**oal from the *Titanic*'s engine room.

◄ **P**edestal for ship's wheel.

▲ **P**assageway lamp.

Brass bell. ►

◄ **G**ilded chandelier from a first-class staircase landing.

▼ **S**hip's compass.

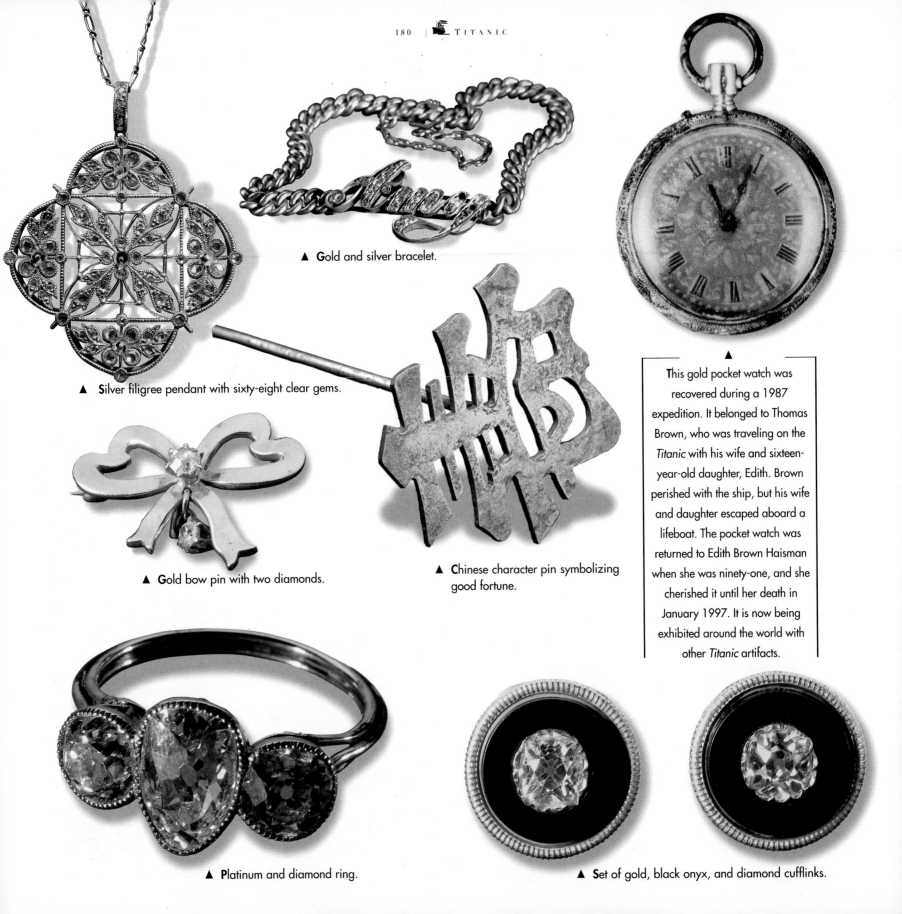

▲ Gold and silver bracelet.

▲ Silver filigree pendant with sixty-eight clear gems.

▲ Gold bow pin with two diamonds.

▲ Chinese character pin symbolizing good fortune.

▲ This gold pocket watch was recovered during a 1987 expedition. It belonged to Thomas Brown, who was traveling on the *Titanic* with his wife and sixteen-year-old daughter, Edith. Brown perished with the ship, but his wife and daughter escaped aboard a lifeboat. The pocket watch was returned to Edith Brown Haisman when she was ninety-one, and she cherished it until her death in January 1997. It is now being exhibited around the world with other *Titanic* artifacts.

▲ Platinum and diamond ring.

▲ Set of gold, black onyx, and diamond cufflinks.

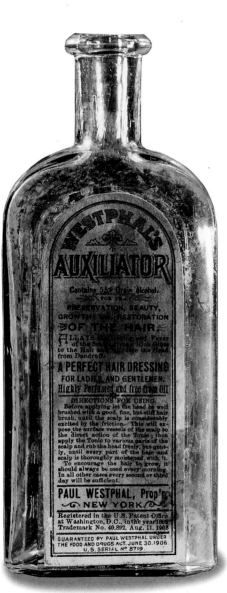

▲ A bottle of hair dressing.

◀ Green glass bottle with cork inside.

◀ Cut crystal carafe.

▲ Glass bottle.

▲ Champagne bottle with cork still in place.

▲ Corked jar of olives.

▲ First-class Spode china plate, cup, and saucer.

◄ Stoneware jug containing seed pits.

▲ Chamber pot.

Third-class soup dish. ▶

▼ Ceramic serving platter.

Miniature souvenir watering can. ▶

A Present from Folkestone.

▲ Silver monogrammed jewelry box.

▲ Leather traveling flask case.

▼ Shoe brush with natural bristle.

◄ Ceramic cold cream jar.

H·P·TRUEFITT
16 OLD BOND STREET
20&21 BURLINGTON ARCADE
AND AT BRIGHTON & ALDER

▲ **A** Waterman self-filling fountain pen.

▲ **S**ilver box containing buttons, cufflinks, and a buckle.

▲ **T**his Steward's cotton jacket was found rolled up into a ball and badly stained by iron corrosion. It was marked with the name "Broome."

◄ **A** Crown Barber's Supply label.

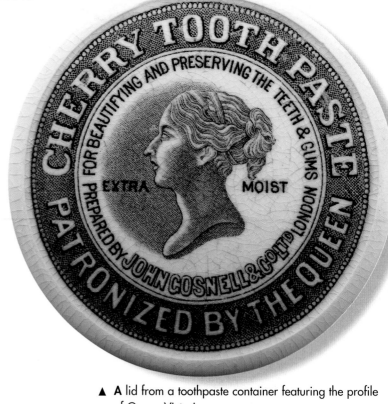

▲ **A** lid from a toothpaste container featuring the profile of Queen Victoria.

◄ Williams shaving stick.

▲ **N**atural bristle shaving brush.

Gillette razor blade envelope.

▲ Bundle of toothpicks.

▲ Steel razor-blade box containing Gillette blades.

▲ Silver-plated safety razor.

EPILOGUE

THE *TITANIC* HAS HELD the interest of people around the world like no other ship in history. Indeed, it is difficult to think of an event, other than political acts of war, terrorism, or assassination, that has so commanded the public's attention for nearly a century. With the passage of years, however, fact and fiction can become easily intertwined. This book is but one element of RMS Titanic, Inc.'s, mission to ensure that the story of the *Titanic* is preserved factually for future generations and shared with the public. The impact and importance of this work, however, are not limited to the chronicling of facts and events. Those who read this volume cannot help but be touched by the experiences of those from all walks of life who enjoyed the grandeur of the *Titanic* and who then suffered the nightmarish events in the dark seas of the North Atlantic.

▲ Quantities of paper have been recovered from the debris field in remarkably good condition. Many items had been stored in leather bags, which protected them from decomposition. New conservation techniques are rendering these papers readable again.

This book is dedicated to the memory of those passengers and crew members who perished. Their lives will also continue to be tangibly remembered through objects that have been recovered from the wreck site, many of which appear in the pages of this book. On a broader scale, present and future generations can also "feel" the magnitude of the tragedy and relate to the human experiences of those aboard the *Titanic* by viewing these recovered objects in public exhibitions.

These objects might never have been available to the public. In the wake of the *Titanic*'s discovery in 1985, there was no plan in place to protect the wreck site or the objects that surrounded the *Titanic* on the ocean floor. To its everlasting credit, IFREMER—the French oceanographic institute that codiscovered the *Titanic* in 1985—recognized the vulnerability of the *Titanic* following its discovery. Lacking funding to recover and protect objects from the *Titanic*, IFREMER sought a partner that had the resources to finance an expedition and that would agree to maintain any artifacts recovered as a collection for public exhibition. A Connecticut group agreed to IFREMER's requirements, risked substantial capital, and chartered IFREMER in 1987 for a research and recovery expedition to the *Titanic*.

This small, original group has grown to become RMS Titanic, Inc., a public company that has been awarded the status of salvor-in-possession of the *Titanic* by order of United States District Court Judge J. Calvitt Clarke, Jr., and is the owner of all the objects recovered from the *Titanic*. During four expeditions, RMS Titanic has recovered nearly five thousand objects from the wreck site. It is an astonishing collection, selected for diversity, message, and voice—ranging from the colossal bitts that secured the *Titanic* during her docking in Southampton, England, to a steward's white linen waistcoat and a passenger's playing cards. These objects speak directly of the people aboard the *Titanic*. All convey the enormity of the human tragedy of the *Titanic*'s sinking and serve as

▶

Survivor Edith Brown Haisman (seated) looks on as fellow survivor Michel Navratil prepares to throw flowers overboard during a memorial at the spot where the *Titanic* sank 84 years earlier. The two were among 1,600 passengers and three survivors who sailed out of New York to the site of the *Titanic*'s sinking aboard the *Island Breeze* on August 27, 1996.

eternal reminders of the memory of those who perished.

Our philosophy at RMS Titanic echoes the thoughts of the *Titanic*'s designer and builder, Thomas Andrews, as he expressed them in his 1910 Christmas card: "It is not what you say, it is not what you think, it is not what you feel. It is what you do." RMS Titanic is dedicated to preserving and protecting the memory of the *Titanic* with dignity and respect. I welcome this opportunity to acknowledge the countless people and institutions around the world who have labored tirelessly in this effort. And, while singling out individuals may seem a disservice to the contributions and sacrifices of so many others, I must recognize my friendship with Commander Paul-Henry Nargeolet, Dr. Stephen Deuchar, Dr. Stéphane Pennec, the late Robert Chappaz, Arnie Geller, Matt Tulloch, the Connecticut partners, historians Charles Haas and Jack Eaton, Michel Stahlberger, and Brad Stillman and Mark Davis, both of whom counseled RMS Titanic through trials over its salvor-in-possession status. And lastly, I want to thank Allan Carlin, my daily colleague, who has been an inspiration to me and to this book and much more than an attorney for RMS Titanic, and my wife, Cindy, whose unfailing support has made it possible for me to give so much of myself to the *Titanic*.

George Tulloch,
President of RMS Titanic, Inc.

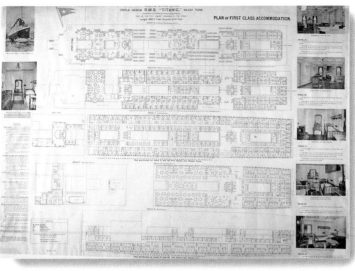

PLAN of FIRST CLASS ACCOMMODATION.

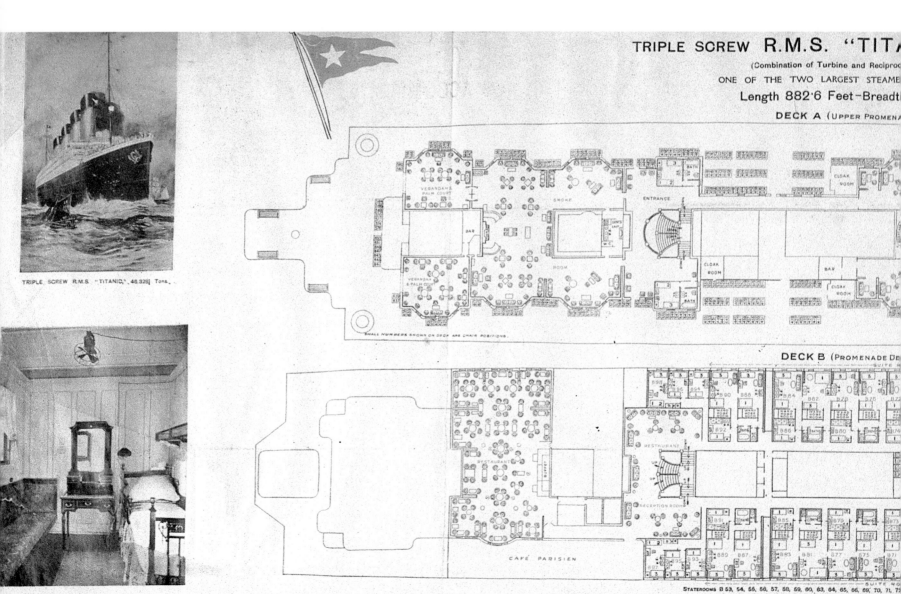

TRIPLE SCREW R.M.S. "TITA

(Combination of Turbine and Reciproc

ONE OF THE TWO LARGEST STEAME

Length 882·6 Feet—Breadth

DECK A (Upper Promena

VERANDAH & PALM COURT

SMOKE ROOM

ENTRANCE

CLOAK ROOM

BATH

BAR

CLOAK ROOM

BAR

CLOAK ROOM

SMALL NUMBERS SHOWN ON DECK ARE CHAIR POSITIONS.

DECK B (PROMENADE DE

RESTAURANT

RECEPTION ROOM

CAFÉ PARISIEN

STATEROOMS B 53, 54, 55, 56, 57, 58, 59, 60, 63, 64, 65, 66, 69, 70, 71,

TRIPLE SCREW R.M.S. "TITANIC," 46,328] Tons.

Single Berth Stateroom A 21 and similar, showing type of Bedstead fitted throughout the First Class Accommodation on Boat Deck and Decks A, B, C and D, and Rooms F 1 to F 42 and F 200 to F 203 on Deck F.

This deck plan, one of only two known to be in existence today, was printed just eleven days before the maiden voyage. The plan, issued by the White Star Line, contains last-minute changes to the *Titanic* and includes the position of every deck chair. The actual size of the plan is roughly 3 feet x 4 feet wide. It is shown in its entirety at left, below, and in the following spread. (Printed with permission of the owner, Stanley Lehrer.)

C," 46,328 TONS.

gines).

THE WORLD

Feet.

K)

PLAN of FIRST CLASS ACCOMMODATION.

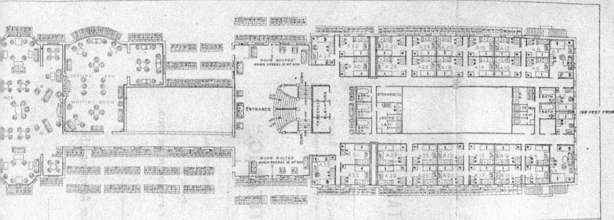

ROOMS A 3 AND 4 ARE FITTED WITH 4 FEET WIDE BEDSTEAD (No. 1).

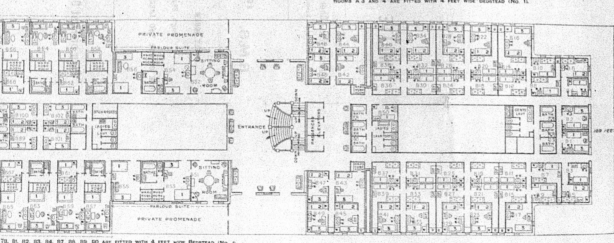

PRIVATE PROMENADE

7, 78, 81, 82, 83, 84, 87, 88, 89, 90 ARE FITTED WITH 4 FEET WIDE BEDSTEAD (No. 2).

BEDROOM OF PARLOUR SUITE

Deck—A.

All Upper Berths (No. 2) in Rooms on this Deck are Pullman Berths and fold up.

Rooms **A** 5, 6, 7, 8, 9, 10, 11, 12, 14, 15, 16, 17, 18, 19, 20, 21, 22, 23, 24, 25, 26, 27, 28, 29, 30, 31, 32 and 33, are so fitted that a Sofa Berth for an extra passenger can be provided when required.

Rooms **A** 5, 6, 9, 10, 14, 15, 18, 19, 22, 23, 26, 27, 30 and 31, are lighted and ventilated from the Deck above (Boat Deck).

SITTING ROOM OF PARLOUR SUITE.

Deck—B.

All Upper Berths (No. 2) in Rooms on this Deck are Pullman Berths and fold up.

Rooms **B** 7, 8, 9, 10, 11, 12, 14, 15, 18, 19, 20, 21, 24, 25, 26, 27, 30, 31, 32, 33, 36, 37, 38 and 39, are so fitted that a Sofa Berth for an extra passenger can be provided when required.

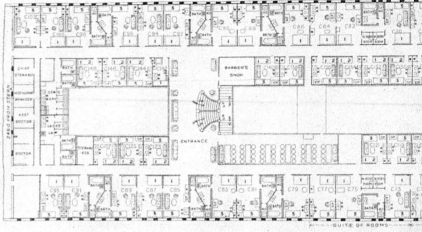

CAFÉ PARISIEN

STATEROOMS B 53, 54, 55, 56, 57, 58, 59, 60, 63, 64, 65, 66, 69, 70,

DECK C (UPPER DECK)
SUITE OF ROOMS

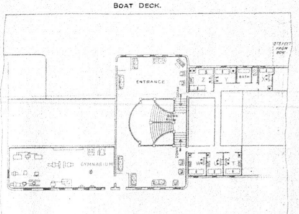

Single Berth Stateroom A 21 and similar, showing type of Bedstead fitted throughout the First Class Accommodation on Boat Deck and Decks A, B, C and D, and Rooms E 1 to E 42, and E 200 to E 203 on Deck E.

NOTES.

RESTAURANT.—In addition to the Regular Dining Saloon there is a large modern à la carte Restaurant, on Deck B, where meals may be obtained at any time between 8 a.m. and 11 p.m. at fixed charges, as shown on the bill of fare issued from day to day.

The Restaurant is under the management of the Company.

If the passage is taken entirely without meals in the regular Dining Saloon, an allowance of £3 per adult will be made off the ocean rate, excepting that on rates of £35 per adult and upwards the allowance will be £5 per adult.

This reduction in fare, however, can only be granted when passengers announce their intention to book without meals, and of making use of the Restaurant, at the time of purchasing their ticket, and so rebate or reduction can be covered under any other circumstances.

Passengers wishing to use the Restaurant should apply on board to the Manager for the reservation of seats.

TURKISH, ELECTRIC AND SWIMMING BATHS.
A fully-equipped Turkish Bath is situated on Deck F, consisting of the usual steam, hot, temperate, shampooing, and cooling rooms. Electric Baths and a Swimming Bath are also provided in conjunction with same, and experienced attendants will be in charge.

These Baths will be available for Ladies from 10 a.m. to 1 p.m.; and for Gentlemen from 2 to 6 p.m., tickets being obtainable at the Enquiry Office at a charge of 4/- (or $1) each.

The Swimming Bath will be open for Gentlemen from 6 to 9 a.m., free of charge.

A GYMNASIUM, fully supplied with modern appliances, is situated on the Boat Deck, and is open for exercise by Ladies and Gentlemen during the same hours as the Baths, no charge being made for the use of the appliances.

The Gymnasium will be available for Children from 1 to 3 p.m. only.

A SQUASH RACQUET COURT is provided on Deck F, and is in charge of a professional player. Tickets for the use of the Court may be obtained at the Enquiry Office at 2/- (or 50 cents) per half hour, to include the services of the Professional if required. Balls may be purchased from the Professional, who is also authorised to sell and hire racquets.

The Court may be reserved in advance by application to the Professional in charge, and may not be occupied for longer than one hour at a time by the same players if others are waiting.

A CLOTHES PRESSING AND CLEANING ROOM is in charge of an expert attendant, who will carry out any work of this kind for Ladies or Gentlemen, in accordance with a fixed printed tariff of charges which can be had on application to the Bedroom Steward.

LOUNGE AND RECEPTION ROOMS.—These rooms are situated on Deck A and at the entrance to the Main Dining Saloon on Deck D respectively. They are intended for the use of both Ladies and Gentlemen, and afternoon tea and after-dinner coffee will be served, while liqueurs, cigars and cigarettes may be purchased there.

Books may be obtained from the Bookcase in the Lounge on Deck A on application to the Steward in charge.

By special arrangement with "The Times" Book Club, a supply of recent works is placed on board each voyage as a supplement to the permanent collection of standard works.

The Lounge will be closed at 11.30 p.m. and the Reception Room at 11 p.m.

PASSENGER ELEVATORS.—There are three elevators provided for the use of Passengers, running between Decks A, B, C, D and E.

VERANDAH CAFÉ AND PALM COURT situated on Deck A, where light refreshments are served.

ELECTRIC HEATERS (under control of passenger) are fitted in all Staterooms on Boat Deck and Decks A, B, C and D, and in Staterooms E 1 to E 64, and E 200 to E 203 on Deck E.

BOAT DECK.

ENTRANCE

GYMNASIUM

STATEROOMS C 57, 59, 61, 63, 64, 65, 66, 67, 68, 69, 70, 71, 72, 73, 74, 75, 76, 77, 78, 79, 80, 81, 82, 83, 84, 85, 86, 87, 88,

The portholes on Deck C are

DECK F (MIDDLE DECK)

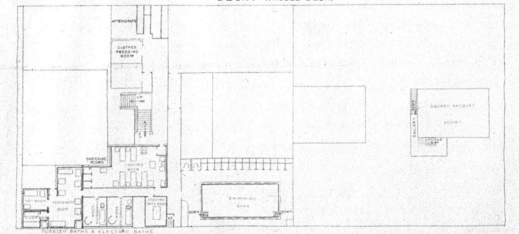

ATTENDANTS

CLOTHES PRESSING ROOM

SQUASH RACQUET COURT

DRESSING ROOMS

COOLING ROOM

SWIMMING BATH

TURKISH BATHS & ELECTRIC BATHS

DECK D (SA

DECK E (MAIN DEC

INDEX.

W.—Indicates Wardrobe.
W.B.— " Wash Basin.
D.T.— " Dressing Table.
D.— " Chest of Drawers.
W.T.— " Writing Table.

All Staterooms on Boat A, B, C, D Decks are fitted with Hot and Cold Water Supply.
Stateroom Numbers in Red.
Berth Numbers in Black.
Odd Numbers are Lower Berths.

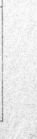

BATH

STATEROOMS WITH BERTHS NUMBERED 1, 2 AND 3 ARE FITTED WITH TWO FIXED BERTHS AND
STATEROOMS E 47, 48, 57, 58, 59, 60, 61, 62, 63 ARE FITTED

MARCH, 1912.

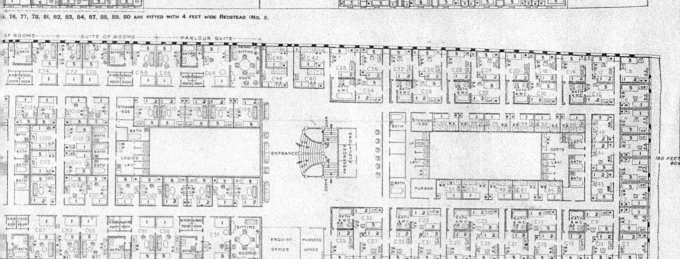

PRIVATE PROMENADE
PARLOUR SUITE
ENTRANCE UP
LADIES LAVY.
SITTING ROOM
109 FEET FROM BOW

, 76, 77, 78, 81, 82, 83, 84, 87, 88, 89, 90 ARE FITTED WITH 4 FEET WIDE BEDSTEAD (No. 2).

OF ROOMS — SUITE OF ROOMS — PARLOUR SUITE
SUITE OF ROOMS — PARLOUR SUITE
SITTING ROOM
ENTRANCE
PASSENGER ELEVATORS
STEWARDESS
PURSER
LADIES LAVY.
GENTS LAVY.
ENQUIRY OFFICE
PURSERS OFFICE
PURSERS ROOMS
180 FEET FROM BOW

, 92, 93, 94, 96, 98, 100, 102 ARE FITTED WITH 4 FEET WIDE BEDSTEAD (No. 1).

feet above the Water Line.

(ECK.)
DINING SALOON
RECEPTION ROOM
ENTRANCE
PASSENGER ELEVATORS
ARCHED OPENING
ARCHED OPENING
LADIES LAVY.
BATH
STEWARDS COR.
ENTRANCE
180 FEET FROM BOW

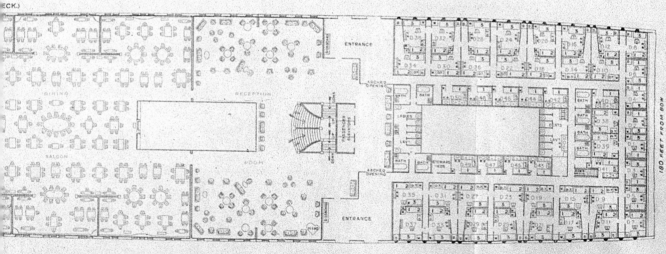

GENTS LAVY.
LADIES LAVY.
BATH
ENTRANCE
PASSENGER ELEVATORS
LADIES LAVY.
ENTRANCE
PROMENADE
BATH
180 FEET FROM BOW
NO. 31.

ED LOWER BERTH (No. 1) AND A PULLMAN UPPER BERTH (No. 2).

STATEROOMS WITH BERTHS NUMBERED 1, 2 AND 3 ARE FITTED WITH TWO BEDSTEADS AND A PULLMAN UPPER BERTH (No. 2).

Deck—B.

All Upper Berths (No. 2) in Rooms on this Deck are Pullman Berths fold up.

Rooms B 7, 8, 9, 10, 11, 12, 14, 15, 18, 19, 20, 21, 24, 25, 26, 27, 31, 32, 33, 36, 37, 38 and 39, are so fitted that a Sofa Berth for an passenger can be provided when required.

STATEROOM B 21 AND SIMILAR.

Deck—C.

All Upper Berths (No. 2) in Rooms on this Deck are Pullman Berth fold up.

Rooms C 1, 2, 3, 4, 5, 6, 45, 47, 49, 50, 51, 52, 53, 54, 56, 58, 60, 9 105, 107, 109, 111, 114, 116, 118, 122 and 124 are so fitted that a P Upper Berth for an extra passenger can be provided when required.

Rooms C 40, 42, 44 and 46 are so fitted that a Sofa Berth for an passenger can be provided when required.

STATEROOM C 9 AND SIMILAR.
Showing Pullman Upper Berth closed.

Deck—D.

All Upper Berths (No. 2) in Rooms on this Deck are Pullman and fold up.

Rooms D 40, 41, 42, 43, 44, 45, 46, 47, 48, 49 and 50 are so fitted Pullman Upper Berth for a second passenger can be provided when requ

INSIDE STATEROOM C 117 AND SIMILAR.

Deck—E.

Rooms E 11, 13, 14, 15, 26, 27, 38, 39, 40, 41 and 42 are so fit

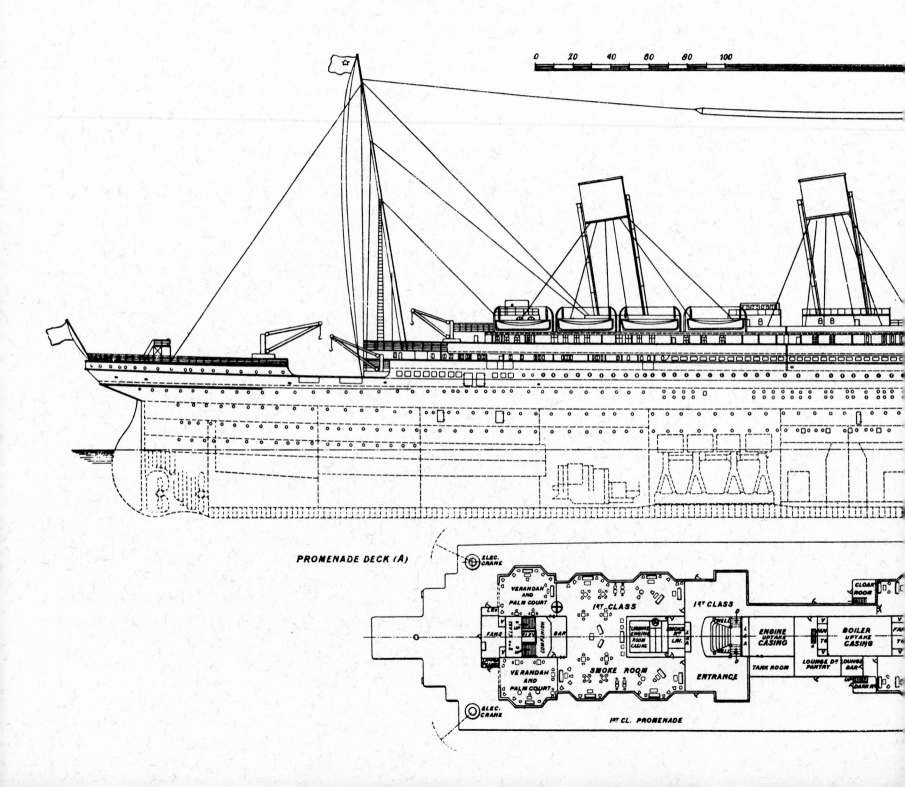

PROMENADE DECK (A)

ELEC.
CRANE

VERANDAH
AND
PALM COURT

1ST CLASS

1ST CLASS

CLOAK
ROOM

TURBINE
ENGINE
ROOM
CASING

SMOKE
R°F
L°N.

WELL

ENGINE
UPTAKE
CASING

BOILER
UPTAKE
CASING

COMPANION

ELEV.

BAR

VERANDAH
AND
PALM COURT

SMOKE ROOM

ENTRANCE

TANK ROOM

LOUNGE D°
PANTRY

LOUNGE
BAR

ELEC.
CRANE

1ST CL. PROMENADE

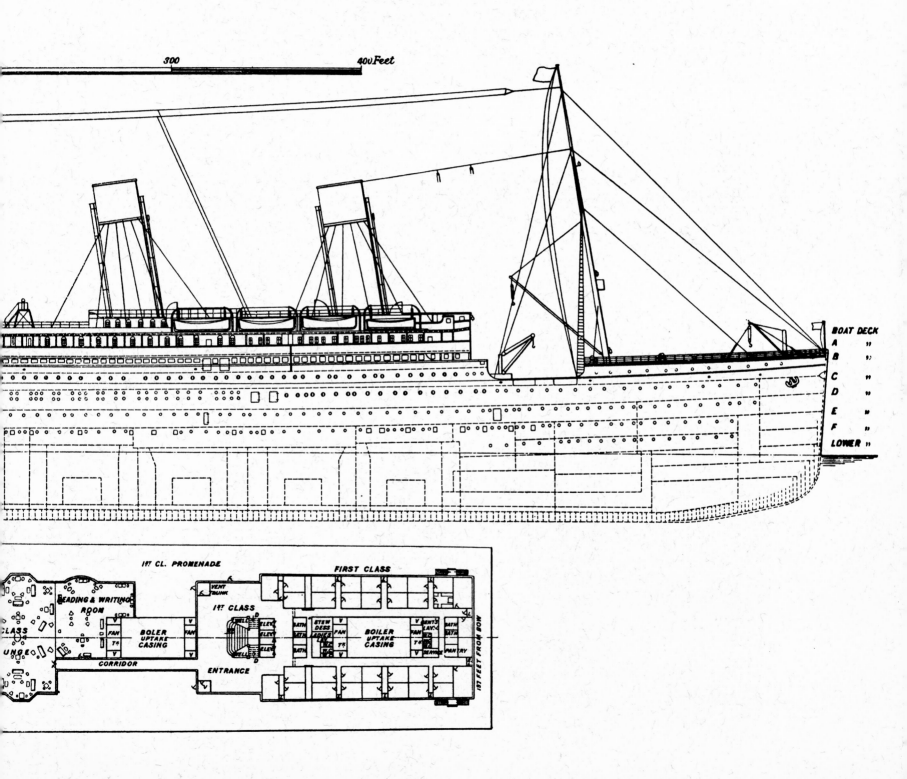

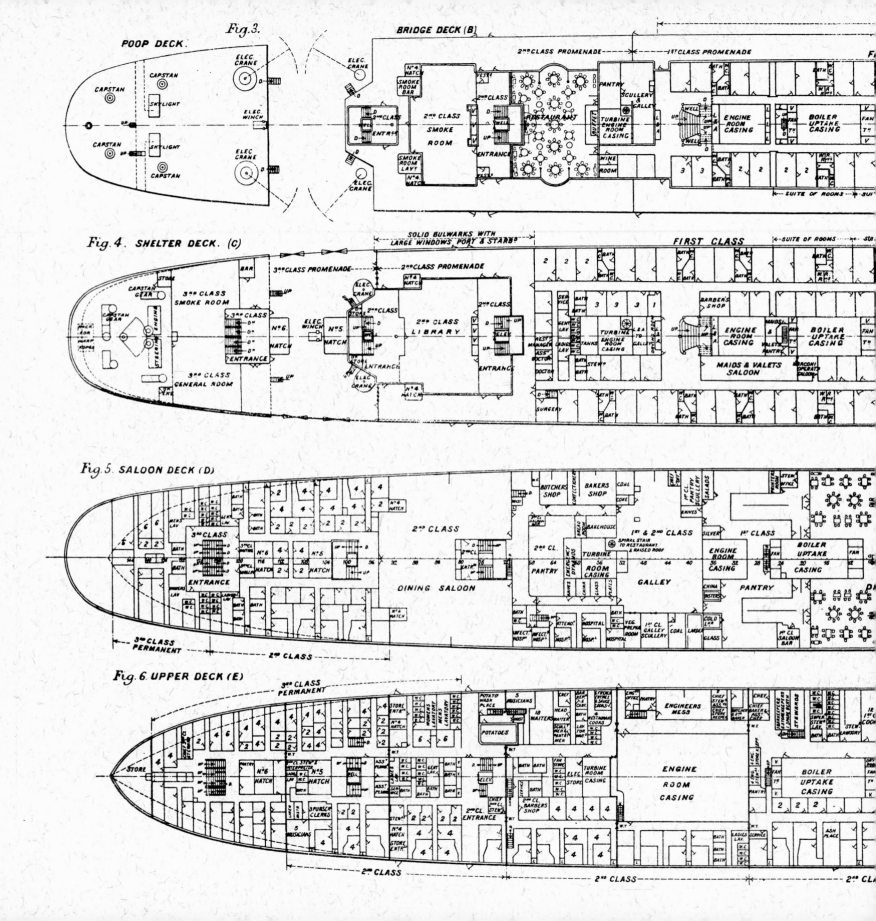

Fig. 3.

POOP DECK.

BRIDGE DECK (B)

2ND CLASS PROMENADE — 1ST CLASS PROMENADE

Fig. 4. SHELTER DECK. (C)

SOLID BULWARKS WITH LARGE WINDOWS PORT & STARB'D

FIRST CLASS — SUITE OF ROOMS

Fig. 5. SALOON DECK (D)

Fig. 6. UPPER DECK (E)

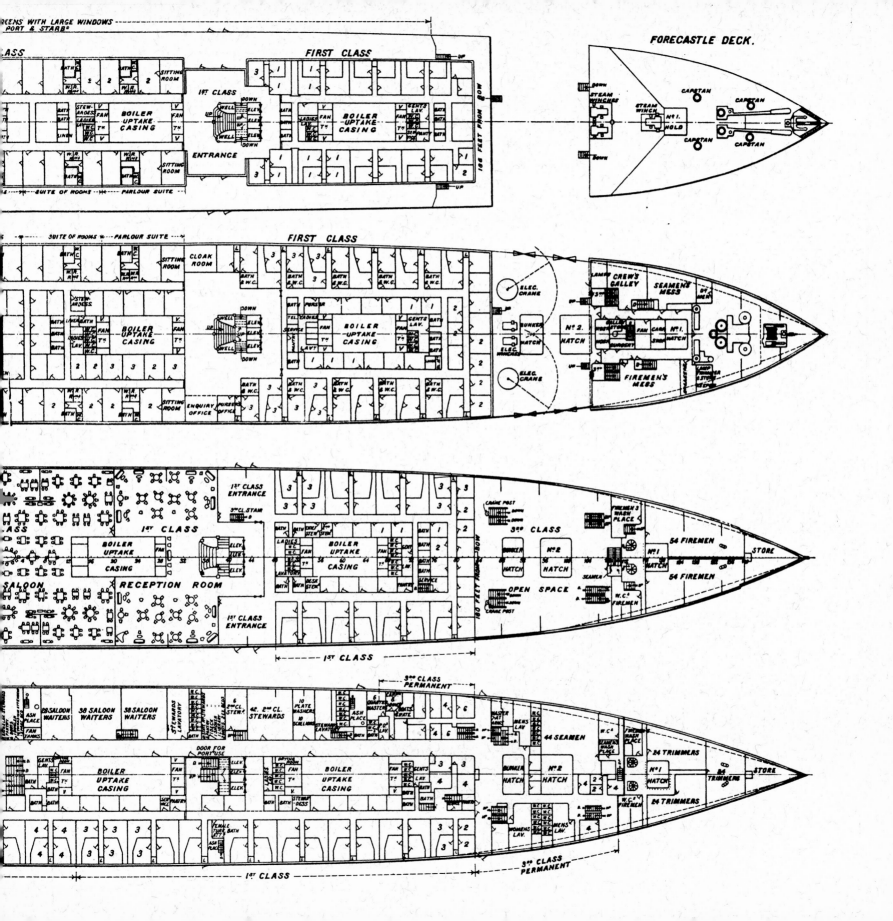

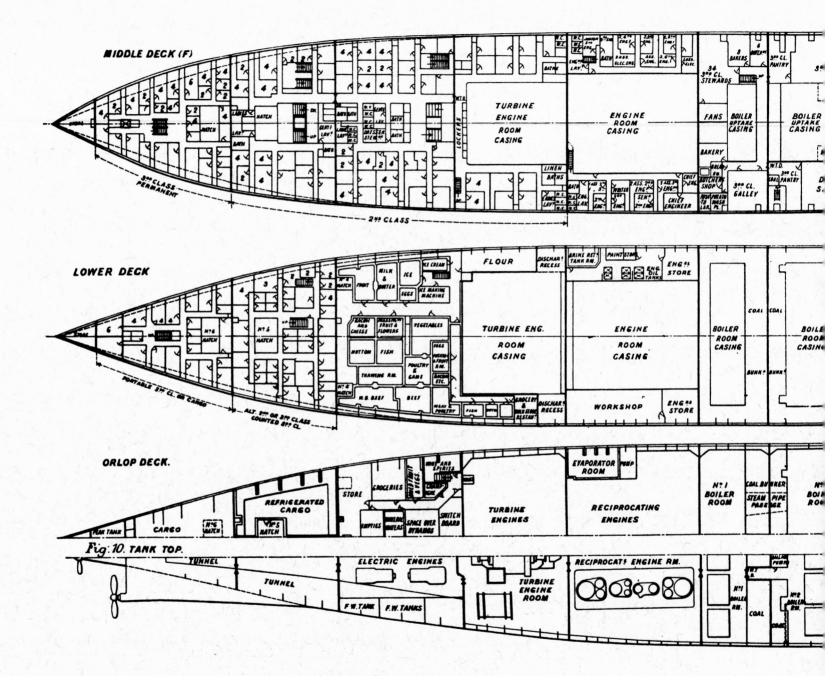

MIDDLE DECK (F)

3RD CLASS PERMANENT

2ND CLASS

TURBINE ENGINE ROOM CASING

ENGINE ROOM CASING

FANS

BOILER UPTAKE CASING

BOILER UPTAKE CASING

3RD CL. STEWARDS

BAKERS

3RD CL. PANTRY

BAKERY

3RD CL. GALLEY

3RD CL. PANTRY

LINEN BATHS

CHIEF ENGINEER

BUTCHERS SHOP

LOWER DECK

PORTABLE 3RD CL. OR CARGO

ALT. 2ND OR 3RD CLASS COUNTED 3RD CL.

MILK & BUTTER

ICE

ICE CREAM

EGGS

ICE MAKING MACHINE

BACON AND CHEESE

DRESSING FRUIT & FLOWERS

VEGETABLES

MUTTON

FISH

POTATO & FRUIT RM.

BACON ETC.

THAWING RM.

POULTRY & GAME

MEAT POULTRY

BEEF

GROCERY & BULK STORE RESTANT

FLOUR

DISCHARG. RECESS

BRINE RET. TANK RM.

PAINT STORE

ENG. OIL TANKS

ENGRS STORE

TURBINE ENG. ROOM CASING

ENGINE ROOM CASING

DISCHARG. RECESS

WORKSHOP

ENGRS STORE

BOILER ROOM CASING

BOILER ROOM CASING

COAL

COAL

BUNKR

BUNKR

ORLOP DECK.

PEAK TANK

CARGO

REFRIGERATED CARGO

STORE

WINE AND SPIRITS

GROCERIES

POTATOES & VEGS

CHAMPAGNE

EMPTIES

WHEAT

SPACE OVER DYNAMOS

SWITCH BOARD

TURBINE ENGINES

RECIPROCATING ENGINES

EVAPORATOR ROOM

PUMP

Nº 1 BOILER ROOM

COAL BUNKER

STEAM PIPE PASSAGE

Nº 2 BOILER ROOM

Fig. 10. TANK TOP.

TUNNEL

TUNNEL

ELECTRIC ENGINES

F.W. TANK

F.W. TANKS

TURBINE ENGINE ROOM

RECIPROCATG. ENGINE RM.

Nº 1 BOILER RM.

COAL

Nº 2 BOILER RM.

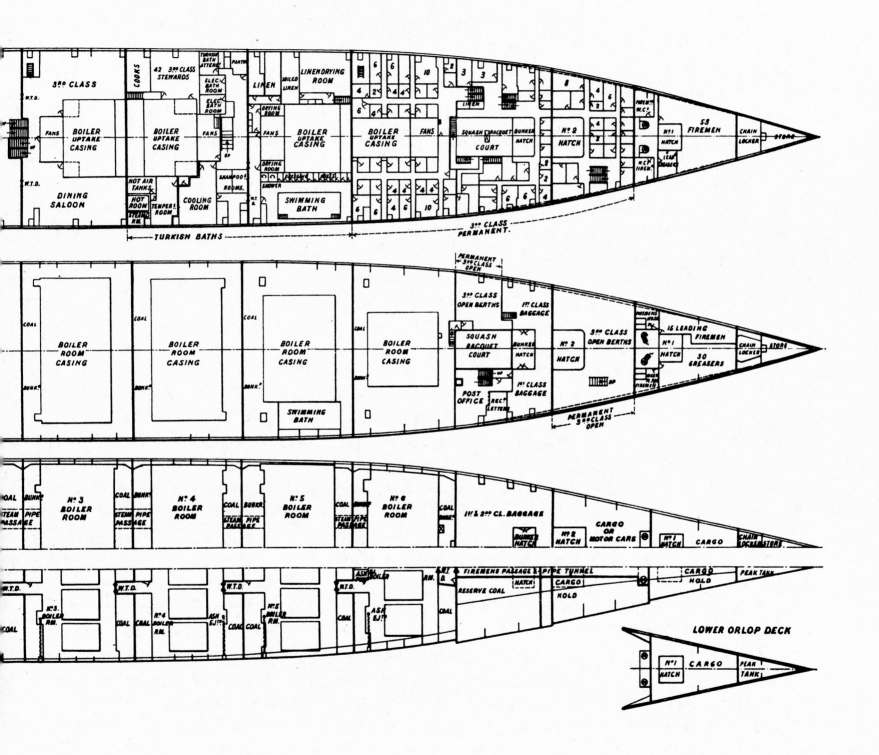

PHOTO CREDITS

Archive Photos: 44a, 45.

Anita Brosius: 111.

Father Francis M. Brown. S. J. Collection: iv, 21, 46a-b, 47, 52b, 53a, 58a, 73, 81a, 81c.

Richard N. Carter: 97, 115, 116d-e, 138-139, 143, 146-147.

Corbis Bettman: xv-xiv, 57f, 85, 89, 90b, 93a, 98a, 99b, 100 (Underwood & Underwood), 101, 102a, 104, 105b (Underwood & Underwood), 107, 112 (UPI), 117 (UPI).

Cyberflix, Inc, rendered images from Titanic: Adventure Out of Time **CD-ROM:** xvii-xvi, 40-41, 62-63, 71.

Michael Findlay: 80a, 82, 83a-b, 83d, 88f, 98b.

Simon Fisher: 14-15, 76-77, 94-95.

James Flood: 92.

Charles Haas Collection: 86a-c.

IMAX Corporation/TMP: vii, 108.

Stanley Lehrer Collection: 29c, 30a, 32a (photo by Michel Friang), 38c, 52a (photo by Michel Friang), 61a-d, 75a-b (photo by Michel Friang), 87c, 90a, 91, 93b, 102, 103b, 192-195 (photo by Michel Friang).

Library of Congress: 17a, 27a, 28, 29a, 31b, 37, 38b, 39a, 65c, 66a, 96, 103a, 105a.

Mariners' Museum, Newport News, Virginia: xix-xviii.

Maritime Museum of the Atlantic, Halifax, Nova Scotia: 53b.

National Geographic Magazine Image Collection: 78 (George Mobley), 113, 114 (Davis Meltzer), 120 (Emory Kristof), 122-123, 124 (Richard Schlect), 127 (William H. Bond).

National Maritime Museum, London: 32b-33, 110, 118-119.

New York Public Library: 59.

Polaris Imaging: 138d, 141a-b, 142.

RMS Titanic Inc.: xiii-xii, xi, x, ix, viii, i, 1*, 2, 3, 5*, 6*, 7b*, 8a-d*, 11, 17b, 27b*, 29d*, 30b, 34a*, 36a, 39b-c*, 43a-d*, 44b*, 49a*, 49b, 57a, 57b-d*, 65a-b*, 66b*, 67b*, 70b, 70f*, 74*, 79, 80b*, 84a, 88a-e*, 109*, 116b, 121a*, 121b, 125, 128, 129a, 129b*, 130, 131*, 133, 134, 135a-b, 136a-b, 137a, 137b*, 138a-c, 138e, 139a-c, 140, 144, 145, 148, 149, 150a, 150b*, 153, 154, 155, 156, 158, 159a, 159b*, 160, 161a*, 161b, 162, 163, 164-165, 166, 167b, 168, 169, 170a*, 173b*, 174b-d*, 175b-c*, 176a-c*, 177a*, 177c*, 178*, 179a-b*, 179c, 180a*, 180g, 181a-e*, 182a-d*, 183a-c*, 184a-e*, 185a-b*, 186a-d*, 187a-b*, 187c, 187d*, 188, 191, 206. (*photos by Philipp Scholz Ritterman)

RMS Titanic Inc. / LP3 Conservation: xxii, 46c, 57e, 58b, 66c, 69a, 70a, 70c, 70d-e, 70g-h, 87a-b, 157, 167a, 170b, 171a-b, 172, 173a, 174a, 175a, 175d, 177b, 179d, 181f, 189.

Steamship Historical Society Collection, University of Baltimore Library: 7, 36b, 38a, 39d.

Ulster Folk & Transport Museum: xxi-xx, iii-ii, 10, 13, 16, 20a, 22a-b, 23, 24-25, 29b, 29e, 31a, 34b-c, 35, 42, 48, 54-55, 56, 60, 64, 67a, 68, 69b, 116c.

Ed Walker: 4, 50-51.

Wetterholm Collection / Harland & Wolff: 18-19, 20b, 72, 84b, 99a.

SELECTED BIBLIOGRAPHY

Abell, Sir Wetcott. *The Safe Sea*. Liverpool: The Journal of Commerce, Charles Birchall, Ltd., 1932.

Ballard, Dr. Robert D. *The Discovery of the Titanic*. Toronto: Madison Press Books, 1987.

Ballard, Dr. Robert D. "A Long Last Look at Titanic." *National Geographic*: Dec. 1986.

Ballard, Dr. Robert D. "How We Found Titanic." *National Geographic*: Dec. 1985.

Bonsall, Thomas E. *Titanic: The Story of the Great White Star Line Trio*. New York: Gallery Books, 1989.

Boyer, Jim. "That Sinking Feeling." *Men's Journal*: February 1997.

Boyer, Jim. "Titanic: Raising a Legend." Discovery Channel Online, 1996. http//www.discovery.com/area/science/titanic/titanicopener.html

Brown, Richard. *Voyage of the Iceberg*. New York: Beaufort Books, 1983.

Candee, Helen Churchill. "Sealed Orders." *Collier's*: May 4, 1912.

Dane, Abe. "A Ghostly Return." *Popular Mechanics*: Aug. 1992.

Davie, Michael. *Titanic*. New York: Alfred A. Knopf, 1987.

Drucker, Peter F. "Technology and Society in the Twentieth Century." *Technology in Western Civilization, Vol. II*. London: Oxford University Press, 1967.

Eaton, John P., and Charles A. Haas. *Titanic: Destination Disaster*. New York: W.W. Norton, 1987.

Eaton, John P., and Charles A. Haas. *Titanic: Triumph and Tragedy*. New York: W.W. Norton, 1994.

Geier, Thom. "Tragic Treasure." *U.S. News & World Report*: Sept. 9, 1996, p. 10.

Gibbs, Commander C. R. Vernon. *Passenger Liners of the Western Ocean*. London: Staples Press, 1952.

Golden, Frederick. "A Man with Titanic Vision." *Discover*: Jan. 1987.

Guthrie, John. *Bizarre Ships of the Nineteenth Century*. South Brunswick and New York: A. S. Barnes and Company, 1970

Haas, Charles A. "A Journey of Time." *Voyage 22, the Journal of Titanic International, Inc.*: Winter 1996.

Hoffman, William, and Jack Grimm. *Beyond Reach: The Search for the Titanic*. New York: Beaufort Books, 1981.

Holmes, Sir George C. V. *Ancient and Modern Ships: Part II. The Era of Steam, Iron & Steel*. London: Wyman & Sons, Victoria and Albert Museum, 1906.

Hutchings, David F. *RMS Titanic: A Modern Legend*. Dorset: Waterfront Publications, 1993.

Hutchinson, Gillian. "Titanic Today." *USA Today*: March 1995, pp. 58-69.

Hyslop, Donald, Alastair Forsyth, and Sheila Jemima. *Titanic Voices*. Southampton: Southampton City Council, 1994.

Inglis, William. "The True Story of the Disaster." *Harper's Weekly*: April 27, 1912.

Kranzberg, Melvin, and Carroll W. Pursell, Jr. "The Promise of Technology for the Twentieth Century." *Technology in Western Civilization, Vol. II*. London: Oxford University Press, 1967.

Lemonick, Michael D. "J. J. Tours the Titanic." *Time*: July 28, 1986.

Lemonick, Michael D. "Tempest over the Titanic." *Time*: Aug. 3, 1987.

Lemonick, Michael D. "Treasures Reclaimed from the Deep." *Time*: Nov. 2, 1987.

Lord, Walter. *The Night Lives On*. New York: William Morrow, 1986.

Lord, Walter. *A Night to Remember*. New York: Holt, Rinehart and Winston, 1955.

Lynch, Don. *Titanic: An Illustrated History*. New York: Hyperion, 1992.

MacInnis, Joe. "An Eerie Graveyard." *Maclean's*: Jan. 27, 1992.

Marcus, Geoffrey. *The Maiden Voyage*. London: New English Library, 1974.

Marschall, Ken. "A Titanic Task." *USA Today*: Nov. 1995.

McDowell, William. *The Shape of Ships*. London: Hutchinson & Co., 1950.

Murphy, Jamie. "Down into the Deep." *Time*: Aug. 11, 1986.

Murphy, Joy Waldron. "The Search for the Titanic Is Over." *Smithsonian*: Aug. 1986.

Pellow, James. *A Lifetime on the* Titanic: *The Biography of Edith Haisman, Britain's Oldest Survivor of the Titanic Disaster*. London: Island Books, 1995.

Powell, Steward. "Journey through the Portholes of a Gilded Past." *U.S. News & World Report*: July 28, 1986.

Priestley, J. B. *The Edwardians*. New York: Harper & Row, 1970.

Reid, Sydney. "The 'Titanic' Disaster." *The Independent*: April 25, 1912.

The White Star Triple Screw Atlantic Liners Olympic and Titanic. New York: Arco Publishing Co., 1970.

Tulloch, Matthew. "North Atlantic Preludes." *Voyage 22, the Journal of Titanic International, Inc.*: Winter 1996.

Twain, Mark. "About All Kinds of Ships." *Collected Tales, Sketches, Speeches, & Essays, 1891–1910*. New York: Library of America, 1992.

Verne, Jules. *A Floating City*. London: Bernard Hamison Ltd., 1958.

Villiers, Alan. *Men, Ships, and the Sea*. Washington, D.C.: National Geographic Society, 1962.

Villiers, Alan. *Wild Ocean: The Story of the North Atlantic and the Men Who Sailed It*. New York: McGraw-Hill, 1957.

Wade, Wyn Craig. *The Titanic: End of a Dream*. London: Penguin Books, 1980.

Wilson-Smith, Anthony. "That Sinking Feeling." *Maclean's*: Sept. 9, 1996.

Winocur, Jack, ed. *The Story of the Titanic as Told by Its Survivors*. New York: Dover Publications, 1960.

Wozniak, Rhonda. "A Place for Miracles." *Voyage 22, the Journal of Titanic International, Inc.*: Winter 1996.

The Economist

The New York Times

The Outlook

INDEX

FIRST SAILING OF THE LATEST ADDITION TO THE WHITE STAR FLEET

The Queen of the Ocean

TITANIC

LENGTH 882½ FT. OVER 45,000 TONS BEAM 92½ FT.
TRIPLE-SCREWS

This, the Latest, Largest and Finest Steamer Afloat, will sail from

WHITE STAR LINE, PIER 59 (North River), NEW YORK

Saturday, April 20th At 12 Noon

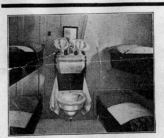

All passengers berthed in closed rooms containing 2, 4, or 6 berths, a large number equipped with washstands, etc.

THIRD CLASS FOUR BERTH ROOM

Spacious Dining Saloons
Smoking Room
Ladies' Reading Room
Covered Promenade

THIRD CLASS DINING SALOON

Reservations of Berths may be made direct with this Office or through any of our accredited Agents

THIRD CLASS RATES ARE:

To PLYMOUTH, SOUTHAMPTON, LONDON, LIVERPOOL and GLASGOW,	$36.25
To GOTHENBURG, MALMÖ, CHRISTIANIA, COPENHAGEN, ESBJERG, Etc. . .	41.50
To STOCKHOLM, ÅBO, HANGÖ, HELSINGFORS	44.50
To HAMBURG, BREMEN, ANTWERP, AMSTERDAM, ROTTERDAM, HAVRE, CHERBOURG	45.00

TURIN, $48. NAPLES, $52.50. PIRAEUS, $55. BEYROUTH, $61, Etc., Etc.

DO NOT DELAY: Secure your tickets through the local Agents or direct from

WHITE STAR LINE, 9 Broadway, New York

TICKETS FOR SALE HERE

CONTINUED FROM BEGINNING OF BOOK

• KEMISH, GEORGE • KEMP, THOMAS • KENCHENTEN, FREDERICK • KENNEDY, JOHN • KENNELL, CHARLES • KENT, EDWARD AUSTIN • KENYON, FREDERICK R. • KENYON, MARION STAUFFER • KENZLER, AUGUSTUS • KERLEY, W. T. • KERR, THOMAS • KETCHLEY, HENRY • KHALIL, BETROS • KHALIL, SAAD • KHALIL, ZAHIE • KIAMIE, ADELE NAJIB • KIERNAN, JAMES W. • KIERNAN, JOHN • KIERNAN, M. • KIERNAN, PHILIP • KILGANNON, THOMAS • KIMBALL, EDWIN NELSON JR. • KIMBALL, GERTRUDE PARSONS • KING, ALFRED • KING, ERNEST WALDRON • KING, GEORGE • KING, THOMAS W. • KINGSCOTE, WILLIAM FORD • KINK, ANTON • KINK, LOUISE GRETCHEN • KINK, LOUISE HEILMANN • KINK, MARIA • KINK, VINCENZ • KINSELLA, L. • KIRKHAM, J. • KIRKLAND, REV. CHARLES LEONARD • KITCHING, A. • KLABER, HERMAN • KLASEN, GERTRUD EMILIA • KLASEN, HULDA KRISTINA • KLASEN, KLAS ALBIN • KLEIN, HERBERT • KNIGHT, GEORGE • KNIGHT, L. • KNIGHT, ROBERT • KNOWLES, T. • KRAEFF, THEODOR • KREKORIAN, NESHAN • KREUCHEN, EMILIE • KRINS, GEORGE ALEXANDER • KVILLNER, JOHAN HENRIK JOHANNESSON • LACEY, BERTRAM W. • LAHOWD, SARKIS • LAHTINEN, ANNA SYLVAN • LAHTINEN, REV. WILLIAM • LAHY, T. • LAITINEN, KRISTINA SOFIA • LAKE, WILLIAM • LALEFF, KRISTO • LAM, ALI • LAM, LEN • LAMB, JOHN JOSEPH • LAMORE, AMELIA (MILLEY) • LANDERGREN, AURORA ADELIA • LANE, A. E. • LANE, PATRICK • LANG, FANG • LAROCHE, JOSEPH PHILIPPE LEMERCIER • LAROCHE, JULIET MARIE LOUISE LAFARGUE • LAROCHE, LOUISE • LAROCHE, SIMONNE MARIE ANNE ANDREE • LARSSON, AUGUST VIKTOR • LARSSON, BENGT EDVIN • LARSSON-RONDBERG, EDVARD • LATIMER, ANDREW • LAUDER, A. • LAVINGTON, BESSIE • LAWRENCE, ARTHUR • LEADER, DR. ALICE FARNHAM • LEATHER, ELIZABETH L. • LEE, H. • LEE, REGINALD ROBINSON • LEENI, FAHIM • LEFEBRE, FRANCES • LEFEBRE, HENRY • LEFEBRE, IDA • LEFEBRE, JEANNIE • LEFÈBRE, MATHILDE • LEFEVRE, GEORGE • LEHMANN, BERTHA • LEINONEN, ANTTI GUSTAF • LEITCH, JESSIE W. • LEMBEROPOLOUS, PETER L. • LEMON, DENIS • LEMON, MARY • LEONARD, LIONEL • LEONARD, MATTHEW • LEROY, BERTHA • LESNEUR, GUSTAVE • LESTER, JAMES • LEVETT, GEORGE ALFRED • LEVY, RENE JACQUES • LEWIS, ARTHUR E. • LEWY, ERWIN G. • LEYSON, ROBERT WILLIAM NORMAN • LIEVENS, RENE • LIGHT, C. • LIGHT, C. • LIGHT, W. • LIGHTOLLER, CHARLES HERBERT • LINDAHL, AGDA V. • LINDBLOM, AUGUSTA CHARLOTTA • LINDEBERG-LIND, ERIK GUSTAF (BOOKED AS MR. EDWARD LINGREY) • LINDELL, EDVARD BENGTSSON • LINDELL, ELIN GERDA • LINDQVIST, EINO WILLIAM • LINDSAY, W. • LINDSTROM, SIGRID POSSE • LINEHAN, MICHAEL • LINES, ELIZABETH LINDSEY JAMES • LINES, MARY CONOVER • LING, LEE • LINGAN, JOHN • LITHMAN, SIMON • LITTLEJOHN, ALEXANDER JAMES • LLOYD, HUMPHREY • LLOYD, W. • LOBB, CORDELIA STANLICK • LOBB, WILLIAM ARTHUR • LOCKE, A. • LOCKYER, EDWARD THOMAS • LONG, F. • LONG, MILTON CLYDE • LONG, W. • LONGLEY, GRETCHEN FISKE • LONGMUIR, JOHN • LORING, JOSEPH HOLLAND • LOUCH, ALICE ADELAIDE • LOUCH, CHARLES ALEXANDER • LOVELL, J. • LOVELL, JOHN HALL • LOWE, HAROLD GODFREY • LUCAS, WILLIAM • LUCAS, WILLIAM • LULICH, NICOLA • LUNDAHL, JOHAN • LUNDIN, OLGA ELIDA • LUNDSTROM, THURE EDVIN • LURETTE, ELISE • LYDIALL, CHARLES • LYNTAKOFF, STANKO • LYONS, WILLIAM HENRY • MABEY, J. • MACK, MARY • MACKAY, CHARLES DONALD • MACKAY, GEORGE WILLIAM • MACKIE, GEORGE WILLIAM • MACKIE, WILLIAM DIXON • MADIGAN, MARGARET • MADILL, GEORGETTE ALEXANDRA • MADSEN, FRITHIOF • MAENPAA, MATTI ALEXANTERI • MAGUIRE, JOHN EDWARD • MAHON, DELIA • MAIONI, RUBERTA • MAISNER, SIMON • MAJOR, ALBERT • MAJOR, E. • MAKINEN, KALLE EDVARD • MALACHARD, NOEL • MALLET, ALBERT • MALLET, ANDRE • MALLET, ANTOINETTE • MAMEE, HANNA • MAMPE, LEON • MANGAN, MARY • MANGIAVACCHI, SERAFINO EMILIO • MANNION, MARGARET • MANSOUR, HANNA • MANTLE, R. • MANTIVILLA, REV. JOSEPH • MARCH, JOHN STARR • MARDIROSIAN, SARKIS • MARECHAL, PIERRE • MARINKO, DMITRI • MARKIM, JOACHIM • MARKOFF, MARIN • MARKS, J. • MARRETT, G. • MARRIOTT, J. W. • MARSDEN, E. • MARSH, FREDERICK CHARLES • MARSHALL, HENRY (IN REALITY, HENRY SAMUEL MORLEY) • MARSHALL, MRS. HENRY (IN REALITY, MISS KATE LOUISE PHILLIPS) • MARTIN, A. • MARTIN, ANNIE • MARTIN, MABEL E. • MARVIN, DANIEL WARNER • MARVIN, MARY GRAHAM FARQUHARSON • MASKELL, LEO ADOLPHUS • MASON, F. • MASON, J. • MASSELMANY, FATIMA • MATHERSON, DAVID • MATHIAS, MONTAGUE VINCENT • MATINOFF, NICOLA • MATTHEWS, WILLIAM JOHN • MATTMAN, ADOLF ICEMAN • MAUGE, PAUL • MAXWELL, JOHN • MAY, ARTHUR • MAY, ARTHUR WILLIAM • MAYBERY, FRANK HUBERT • MAYNARD, JOHN • MAYO, WILLIAM • MAYTUM, ALFRED • MAYZES, A. • MCANDREWS, THOMAS • MCANDREWS, WILLIAM • MCCAFFRY, THOMAS FRANCIS • MCCARTHY, FREDERICK J. • MCCARTHY, KATIE • MCCARTHY, TIMOTHY J. • MCCARTHY, W. • MCCASTLIN, W. • MCCAWLEY, T. W. • MCCORMACK, THOMAS J. • MCCOY, AGNES • MCCOY, ALICE • MCCOY, BERNARD • MCCRAE, ARTHUR GORDON • MCCRIE, JAMES MATTHEW • MCDERMOTT, BRIDGET DELIA • MCELROY, HUGH WALTER • MCELROY, MICHAEL • MCGANN, JAMES • MCGARVEY, EDWARD • MCGAW, ERROLL • MCGOUGH, GEORGE M. • MCGOUGH, JAMES R. • MCGOVERN, MARY • MCGOWAN, ANNIE • MCGOWAN, KATHERINE • MCGRADY, JAMES • MCGREGOR, J. • MCINERNEY, THOMAS • MCINTYRE, WILLIAM • MCKAIN, PETER DAVID • MCKAY, GEORGE WILLIAM • MCLAREN, H. • MCMAHON, MARTIN • MCMIKEN, ALFRED • MCMULLEN, J. • MCMURRAY, WILLIAM • MCNAMEE, EILEEN O'LEARY • MCNAMEE, NEAL • MCQUILLAN, WILLIAM • MCRAE, WILLIAM ALEXANDER • MCREYNOLDS, WILLIAM • MEANWELL, MARION OGDEN • MECHAN, JOHN • MEEK, ANNIE L. • MELKEBUK, PHILEMON • MELLENGER, ELIZABETH ANNE MAIDMENT • MELLENGER, MADELEINE VIOLET • MELLOR, A. • MELLOR, WILLIAM JOHN • MEO, ALFONSO • MEYER, AUGUST • MEYER, EDGAR JOSEPH • MEYER, LEILA SAKS • MIDDLETON, ALFRED PIRRIE • MIDDLETON, M. V. • MIDTSJO, KARL ALBERT • MIHOFF, STOYTCHO • MILES, FRANK • MILFORD, GEORGE • MILLAR, ROBERT • MILLAR, THOMAS • MILLET, FRANCIS DAVIS • MILLING, JACOB CHRISTIAN • MILLS, C. • MINAHAN, DAISY E. • MINAHAN, DR. WILLIAM EDWARD • MINAHAN, LILLIAN E. THORPE • MINEFF, IVAN • MINKOFF, LAZAR • MINTRAM, W. • MIRKO, DIKA • MIRKOFF, MITO • MISHELLANY, ALBERT • MITCHELL, HENRY MICHAEL • MITCHELL, LAWRENCE • MOCK, PHILIP E. • MOCKLARE, HELEN MARY • MOEN, SIGURD HANSEN • MOLSON, HARRY MARKLAND • MONOROS, JEAN • MONTEVERDI, GIOVANNI • MOODY, JAMES PAUL • MOORE, ALFRED E. • MOORE, BELLA • MOORE, CLARENCE BLOOMFIELD • MOORE, GEORGE • MOORE, J. J. • MOORE, LEONARD CHARLES • MOORE, MEYER • MOORE, R. • MOORES, RICHARD HENRY • MORAN, BERTHA • MORAN, DANIEL J. • MORAN, JAMES • MORAWECK, DR. ERNEST • MORGAN, A. H. • MORGAN, C. F. • MORGAN, THOMAS • MORLEY, WILLIAM • MORRELL, R. • MORRIS, A. • MORRIS, FRANK HERBERT • MORRIS, W. • MORROW, THOMAS ROWAN • MOSS, ALBERT JOHAN • MOSS, WILLIAM • MOUBAREK, AMENIA ALEXANDER • MOUBAREK, GEORGE • MOUBAREK, HANNA • MOUBAREK, WILLIAM GEORGE • MOUSSA, MRS. MANTOURA BALOICS • MOUTAL, RAHAMIN HAIM • MOUTAL, RAHAMIN • MOYES, WILLIAM YOUNG • MUDD, THOMAS CHARLES • MULLER, L. • MULLIN, THOMAS A. • MULLINS, KATIE • MULVIHILL, BERTHA E. • MURDLIN, JOSEPH • MURDOCH, WILLIAM MCMASTER • MURDOCK, WILLIAM • MURPHY, JAMES ROBERT* • MURPHY, KATHERINE • MURPHY, MARGARET • MURPHY, NORAH • MYHRMAN, PER FABIAN OLIVER MALKOLM • MYLES, THOMAS FRANCIS • NAHIL, TOUFIK • NAIDENOFF, PENKO • NAKED (NACKID), MARY • NAKED (NACKID), SAID • NAKED (NACKID), MARY MOWAD • NANCARROW, WILLIAM HENRY • NANKOFF, MINKO • NANNINI, FRANCISCO • NASR, MUSTAFA • NASR, SAAD JEAN • NASSER (NASRALLAH), ADELE • NASSER (NASRALLAH), NICHOLAS • NATSCH, CHARLES H. • NAUGHTON, HANNAH • NEAL, H. • NEMAUGH, ROBERT • NENKOFF, CHRISTO • NESSON, ISRAEL • NETTLETON, GEORGE • NEWELL, ARTHUR WEBSTER • NEWELL, MADELEINE • NEWELL, MARJORIE • NEWMAN, CHARLES • NEWSOM, HELEN MONYPENY • NICHOLLS, JOSEPH CHARLES • NICHOLS, A. • NICHOLS, A. D. • NICHOLS, T. • NICHOLS,

THE PASSENGERS AND CREW OF THE TITANIC

WALTER H. • NICHOLSON, ARTHUR ERNEST • NICOLA (YARRED), JAMILA • NICOLA (YARRED), ELIAS • NIEMINEN, MANTA JOSEFINA • NIKLASSON, SAMUEL • NILSSON, AUGUST FERDINAND • NILSSON, HELMINA JOSEFINA • NILSSON, MERTA OLIVIA • NISKANEN, JOHAN • NOON, JOHN • NORMAN, ROBERT DOUGLAS • NOSS, B. • NOSS, HENRY • NOSWORTHY, RICHARD CATER • NOVEL, MANSOUR • NUTBEAN, WILLIAM • NYE, ELIZABETH RAMELL • NYSTEN, ANNA • NYSVEEN, JOHANNES H. • ODAHL, NILS MARTIN • OHMAN, VELIN • OLIVA Y OCANA, FERMINA • OLIVE, CHARLES • OLIVE, ERNEST R. • OLIVER, H. • OLLIVER, ALFRED • OLSEN, ARTHUR • OLSEN, CARL • OLSEN, HENRY MARGIDO • OLSEN, OLE M. • OLSSON, ELIDA • OLSSON, NILS JOHAN • OLSSON, OSCAR JOHANSSON • OLSVIGEN, THOR ANDERSEN • ORESKOVIC, JEKO • ORESKOVIC, LUKA • ORESKOVIC, MARIA • OROVELLO, LOUIS • ORPET, W. H. • ORR, J. • OSBOURNE, W. • OSEN, OLOF ELON • OSMAN, FRANK • OSMAN, MARIA • OSTBY, ENGELHART CORNELIUS • OSTBY, HELEN RAGHNILD • OTHEN, CHARLES • OTTER, RICHARD • OVIES Y RODRIGUEZ, SERVANDO • OWEN, L. • OXENHAM, PERCY THOMAS • O'BRIEN, DENIS • O'BRIEN, HANNAH GODFREY • O'BRIEN, THOMAS • O'CONNELL, PATRICK D. • O'CONNOR, JOHN • O'CONNOR, MAURICE • O'CONNOR, PATRICK • O'CONNOR, THOMAS • O'DWYER, NELLIE • O'KEEFE, PATRICK • O'LEARY, NORAH • O'LOUGHLIN DR. WILLIAM FRANCIS NORMAN • O'NEILL, BRIDGET • O'SULLIVAN, BRIDGET • PACEY, R. J. • PACHERAT, JEAN • PADRO Y MANENT, JULIAN • PAICE, RICHARD • PAIN, DR. ALFRED • PAINTER, CHARLES • PAINTER, FRANK • PAINTIN, JAMES ARTHUR • PALLAS Y CASTILLO, EMILIO • PALLES, T. • PANULA, ERNESTI ARVID • PANULA, JAAKKO ARNÓLD • PANULA, JUHA NIILO • PANULA, MARIA EMILIA • PANULA, WILLIAM • PARKER, CLIFFORD RICHARD • PARKER, T. • PARKES, FRANK • PARR, WILLIAM HENRY MARSH • PARRISH, LUTIE DAVIS • PARSONS, EDWARD • PARSONS, FRANK ALFRED • PARSONS, R. • PARTNER, AUSTIN • PASCOE, C. H. • PASIC, JAKOB • PATCHETT, GEORGE • PAULNER, USCHER • PAULSSON, ALMA CORNELIA BERGLUND • PAULSSON, GOSTA LEONARD • PAULSSON, PAUL FOLKE • PAULSSON, STINA VIOLA • PAULSSON, TORBORG DANIRA • PAVLOVIC, STEFO • PAYNE, VIVIAN ARTHUR PONSONBY • PEACOCK, ALFRED EDWARD • PEACOCK, EDITH TREASTEALL NILE • PEACOCK, TREASTEALL • PEARCE, A. • PEARCE, ERNEST • PEARCE, J. • PEARCEY, ALBERT VICTOR • PEARS, EDITH WEARNE • PEARS, THOMAS • PECRUIC, MATE • PECRUIC, TOME • PEDERSEN, OLAF • PEDRINI, ALBERTO • PEDUZZI, JOSEPH • PEKONIEMI, EDVARD • PELHAM, GEORGE • PELTOMAKI, NIKOLAI JOHANNES • PENASCO, JOSEFA PEREZ deSOTO • PENASCO, VICTOR DE SATODE • PENGELLY, FREDERICK WILLIAM • PENNAL, FREDERICK • PENNY, WILLIAM C. • PENROSE, JOHN P. • PERKIN, JOHN HENRY • PERKINS, L. • PERKIS, WALTER JOHN • PERNOT, RENE • PEROTTI, ALFONSO • PERRACCHIO, ALBERT • PERRACCHIO, SEBASTINE • PERREAULT, ANNE • PERRIN, W. • PERRITON, H. • PERRY, E. • PERSSON, ERNST ULRIK • PERUSCHITZ, REV. JOSEPH M. • PETER (JOSEPH), MARY • PETER (JOSEPH), MICHAEL • PETER (JOSEPH), CATHERINE • PETERS, KATIE • PETERS, W. C. • PETERSEN, MARIUS • PETRANEC, MATILDA • PETROFF, NEDECA • PETROFF, PENTCHO • PETTERSSON, ELLEN NATALIA • PETTERSSON, JOHAN EMIL • PETTY, EDWIN HENRY • PEUCHEN, MAJOR ARTHUR GODFREY • PHILLIMORE, HAROLD • PHILLIPS, ALICE CAROLINE • PHILLIPS, G. • PHILLIPS, J. • PHILLIPS, JOHN GEORGE (JACK) • PHILLIPS, ROBERT • PIATTI, LOUIS • PIAZZA, POMPEO • PICKARD, BERK (TREMBISKY) • PINSKY, ROSA • PITFIELD, WILLIAM JAMES • PITMAN, HERBERT JOHN • PLATT, W. • PLOTCHARSKY, VASIL • PODESTA, JOHN • POGGI, E. • POIGNDESTRE, JOHN • POIRAVANTI, BERTOLDI • POND, C. • PONESELL, MARTIN • POOK, R. • PORT, F. • PORTALUPPI, EMILIO • PORTER, WALTER CHAMBERLAIN • POTTER, LILY ALEXENIA WILSON • PRANGNELL, GEORGE • PRENTICE, FRANK W. • PRESTON, THOMAS CHARLES ALFRED • PRICE, ERNEST • PRIDEAUX, J. W. • PRIEST, JOHN • PRIOR, H. J. • PRITCHARD, A. • PROCTOR, CHARLES • PROFFER, RICHARD • PROUDFOOT, R. • PRYCE, WILLIAM • PUGH, ALFRED • PUGH, PERCY • PULBAUM, FRANZ • PUSEY, ROBERT WILLIAM • PUZEY, JOHN E. • QUICK, JANE RICHARDS • QUICK, PHYLLIS MAY • QUICK, VERA WINNIFRED • RABID, RAZI • RADEFF, ALEXANDER • RANDALL, F. H. • RANGER, THOMAS G. • RANSOM, JAMES • RATTI, ENRICO • RAY, FREDERICK DENT • READ, J. • REED, CHARLES • REED, JAMES GEORGE • REED, ROBERT • REEVES, DAVID • REEVES, F. • REGHINI, SANTE • RENOUF, LILLIAN JEFFEREYS • RENOUF, PETER HENRY • REUCHLIN, JONKHEER JOHN GEORGE • REVELL, W. • REYNALDO, MRS. ENCARNACION • REYNOLDS, HAROLD J. • RHEIMS, GEORGE LUCIEN • RICADONE, RINALDO • RICE, ALBERT • RICE, ARTHUR • RICE, CHARLES • RICE, ERIC • RICE, EUGENE • RICE, GEORGE • RICE, JOHN REGINALD • RICE, MARGARET NORTON • RICE, P. • RICHARD, EMILE • RICHARDS, EMILY HOCKING • RICHARDS, JOSEPH • RICHARDS, WILLIAM ROWE • RICHARDS, SIBLEY GEORGE • RICKMAN, G. • RICKS, CYRIL G. • RIDOUT, W. • RIDSDALE, LUCY • RIGOZZI, ABELE • RIIHIIVUORI, SANNI • RINTAMAKI, MATTI • RIORDAN, HANNAH • RISIEN, EMMA • RISIEN, SAMUEL • ROBBINS, VICTOR • ROBERT, ELISABETH WALTON McMILLAN • ROBERTS, FREDERICK • ROBERTS, GEORGE • ROBERTS, HUGH H. • ROBERTS, MARY K. • ROBERTSON, W. GEORGE • ROBINS, ALEXANDER A. • ROBINS, GRACE CHARITY LAWRY • ROBINSON, ANNIE • ROBINSON, JAMES WILLIAM • ROEBLING, WASHINGTON AUGUSTUS II • ROGERS, EDWARD JAMES WILLIAM • ROGERS, HARRY • ROGERS, M. • ROGERS, WILLIAM JOHN • ROMAINE, CHARLES HALLIS • ROMMETVEDT, KARL KRISTIAN KNUT • ROOD, HUGH R. • ROSBLOM, HELEN WILHELMINA • ROSBLOM, SALLI HELENA • ROSBLOM, VIKTOR RICKARD • ROSENBAUM (RUSSELL), EDITH LOUISE • ROSENSHINE, GEORGE • ROSS, H. • ROSS, JOHN HUGO • ROTH, SARAH • ROTHES, THE COUNTESS OF (NOEL LUCY MARTHA-DYER-EDWARDS) • ROTHSCHILD, ELIZABETH L. BARRETT • ROTHSCHILD, MARTIN • ROTTA, ANGELO • ROUS, ARTHUR J. • ROUSE, RICHARD HENRY • ROUSSEAU, P. • ROWE, ALFRED • ROWE, GEORGE THOMAS • ROWE, M. • RUDD, HENRY • RUGG, EMILY • RULE, SAMUEL JAMES • RUMMER, S. • RUSH, ALFRED GEORGE JOHN • RUSSELL, BOYSIE RICHARD • RYAN, EDWARD • RYAN, PATRICK • RYAN, T. • RYERSON, ARTHUR LARNED • RYERSON, EMILY BORIE • RYERSON, EMILY MARIA BORIE • RYERSON, JOHN (JACK) BORIE • RYERSON, SUSETTE PARKER • RYERSON, WILLIAM EDWY • SAAD, AMIN • SAALFELD, ADOLPH • SACCAGGI, GIOVANNI • SADLIER, MATTHEW • SADOWITZ, HARRY • SAETER, SIMON SIVERTSEN • SAGE, ADA • SAGE, ANNIE BULLEN • SAGE, CONSTANCE GLADYS • SAGE, DOROTHY EDITH (DOLLY) • SAGE, DOUGLAS BULLEN • SAGE, FREDERICK • SAGE, GEORGE JOHN • SAGE, JOHN GEORGE • SAGE, STELLA ANNA • SAGE, THOMAS HENRY • SAGE, WILLIAM HENRY • SAGESSER, EMMA • SALANDER, KARL JOHAN • SALKJELSVIK, ANNA KRISTINE • SALOMON, ABRAHAM L. • SALONEN, JOHAN WERNER • SALOSOLLIA, GIOVENEZ • SAMAAN, ELIAS • SAMAAN, HANNA • SAMAAN, YOUSSEF • SAMUEL, O. W. • SANDSTROM, AGNES CHARLOTTA BENGTSSON • SANDSTROM, BEATRICE IRENE • SANDSTROM, MISS MARGURITE RUT • SANGSTER, C. • SAP, JULES • SAUNDERCOCK, WILLIAM HENRY • SAUNDERS, D. E. • SAUNDERS, F. • SAUNDERS, W. • SAUNDERS, W. • SAVAGE, C. J. • SAWYER, FREDERICK CHARLES • SAWYER, ROBERT • SCANLON, JAMES • SCARRETT, JOSEPH • SCAVINO, C. • SCHABERT, EMMA MOCK • SCHEERLINCKX, JEAN • SCOTT, ARCHIBALD • SCOTT, FREDERICK • SCOTT, J. • SCOTT, SAMUEL JOSEPH* • SCOVELL, ROBERT • SDYCOFF, TODOR • SEDGWICK, CHARLES FREDERICK WADDINGTON • SEDUNARY, SIDNEY FRANCIS 2ND • SELF, ALFRED HENRY • SELF, E. • SEMAN, BETROS • SENIOR, HARRY • SEREPECA, AUGUSTA • SESIA, GINO • SEVIER, W. • SEWARD, FREDERIC KIMBER • SEWARD, WILFRED DEEBLE • SHARP, PERCIVAL JAMES • SHAUGHNESAY, PATRICK • SHAW, HARRY • SHEA, JOHN • SHEA, THOMAS • SHEATH, FREDERICK • SHEDID, DAHER • SHELLARD, FREDERICK BLAINEY • SHELLEY, IMANITA HALL • SHEPHERD, JONATHAN • SHILLABER, CHARLES • SHINE, ELLEN • SHIRES, ALFRED • SHORNEY, CHARLES JOSEPH • SHUTES, ELIZABETH W. • SIEBERT, SIDNEY CONRAD • SILVEN, LYYLI • SILVERTHORNE, SPENCER VICTOR • SILVEY, ALICE MUNGER • SILVEY, WILLIAM BAIRD • SIMMONDS, A. • SIMMONDS, F. C. • SIMMONDS, W.P • SIMMONS, JOHN • SIMONIUS-BLUMER,